AIR RIFLES

A BUYER'S AND SHOOTER'S GUIDE

by

STEVE MARKWITH

Part of the *Survival Guns* series of books
published by:

Prepper Press
Your Survival Library

PrepperPress.com/SurvivalGuns

ISBN 13: 978-0-615-46506-7

Printed in the United States of America.

Prepper Press Paperback Edition: September 2015

Prepper Press is a division of Kennebec Publishing, LLC

Special thanks to Pyramyd Air for their cooperation in lending photographs to help complete this book.

Disclaimer. This book is intended to offer general guidance relating to firearms. It is sold with the understanding that every effort was made to provide accurate information; however, errors are still possible. The author and publisher make no warrantees or claims as to the truth or validity of the information. The author and publisher shall have neither liability nor responsibility to any person or entity over any loss or damage caused, or alleged to have been caused, directly or indirectly, by the information contained within this book.

ABOUT THE AUTHOR

Steve has a lifelong interest in just about all things that shoot including rifles, shotguns, revolvers, pistols, air guns, and black powder guns, as well as vertical or horizontal bows. He began formal firearms training at age 11 during NRA-sanctioned small-bore target rifle events, and was an active hunter by the age of 12. He began reloading shotgun shells at 14, using a handheld Lee Loader to feed his addiction. After joining the U.S. Army, he served two combat tours in Vietnam, gaining experience with numerous military firearms during Air Cavalry helicopter operations and ground-based reconnaissance missions.

Upon returning to civilian life, Steve resumed shooting, participating in NRA bullseye, combat pistol, and trap events. These activities expanded his reloading experience to metallic ammunition and bullet casting. Steve eventually became an NRA-certified pistol, rifle & shotgun instructor, as well as a certifying official for state firearms permit applicants. He also worked for a well-known gunsmith and PO Ackley disciple, until an untimely death forced a career change.

Joining a major state correctional agency, Steve was soon appointed as a firearms instructor, eventually assuming control of all state correctional firearms operations. He's still working, and holds a master instructor rating, plus numerous other federal, state, and industry certifications. He has over 25 years of full-time firearms training experience, and many industry connections.

Steve also has extensive hunting experience in the Northeast, and at other locations throughout the United States. He holds an archery deer record, and actively remains afield on a year-round basis, whether chasing spring turkeys or winter coyotes with night-vision equipped AR-15s. He also writes when time permits, and has had numerous articles published about firearms and the great outdoors.

Steve has been actively shooting airguns since his preteen years. He was well-positioned to witness the remarkable growth of air-powered technologies, beginning with the introduction of sophisticated European and British imports during the mid-1970s. Steve was among the first to make the early jump, and has been an active participant ever since. Whether engaged in pest control shoots or scaled precision rifle events, odds are he'll have a host of interesting airguns close at hand.

Disclaimer. This book is intended to offer general guidance relating to firearms. It is sold with the understanding that every effort was made to provide accurate information; however, errors are still possible. The author and publisher make no warrantees or claims as to the truth or validity of the information. The author and publisher shall have neither liability nor responsibility to any person or entity over any loss or damage caused, or alleged to have been caused, directly or indirectly, by the information contained within this book.

PREFACE

I carefully maneuvered a hard shell rifle case through the series of heavy, barred doors that isolated a maximum security prison from the outside world. The last steel barrier clanged shut with a loud metallic bang, and I was inside The Big House. My destination was the prison yard, a spot that made a good vantage point for the task at hand. There was little time to waste. The rifle was uncased in preparation for the shot. A railing provided some stability and, when the crosshairs settled on the mark, I carefully squeezed off a round. The reaction was instantaneous, resulting in a three-story plummet to the ball field below. I reloaded and lined up on another target to my right. The report was muffled, but the hard smack of the projectile was clearly audible. The process was repeated twenty-four more times. Operation Jailbird was in full swing.

An unwelcome group of residents had moved into the State Prison. They weren't stool pigeons - just the plain, feathered nuisance variety. It was obvious they planned on doing life while living large on mess hall scraps. They tucked into the nooks and crannies of the imposing old brick fortress... and bred. The population rapidly grew, and there was unrest in the realm. Staff and inmates alike ducked droppings during their daily goings about. Hygiene became a concern, and *something* needed to be done.

A plastic great horned owl was deputized to stand watch over the prison yard. Before long, a pigeon alighted on a wire above and pooped on its head. The reputation of the higher-ups was sullied. The inmates found it amusing. Clearly, the feathered jailbirds required a stiffer sentence. I got a call. Did I have a quiet means for surgical elimination of the problem? Why yes, as a matter of fact, I did.

The inmates were routinely confined to their cells every Saturday evening. This respite provided a short summer window of just two hours in which to do some outdoor shooting. So, in I went with a .22 caliber RWS Model 48 air rifle. Truthfully, I wasn't sure how well the whole thing would work. Perhaps I might shoot three or four of our feathered miscreants, but large-scale results seemed iffy.

Boy, was I wrong! The sun was low on the horizon when I decided to quit shooting. The large "Hefty" body bag that contained twenty-five victims was barely portable. I packed up and was about to exit the facility when an officer bet me a dollar I couldn't shoot Number 26, who was perched on a second story railing. An indoor church service was in full swing only ten feet to my left, but securely isolated within the confines of the old chapel. It seemed like a chance to make an easy buck, so I uncased the rifle. A hymn was in progress and, when the inmates hit a high note, I squeezed off a shot. Number 26 was in the bag, along with my dollar. Thanks to some good Teutonic technology, nobody ever knew the difference. Four more trips resulted in 100 pigeons that just "disappeared". Operation Jailbird was complete.

During worse times, the setting might be an old fac-tory or barn. Get hungry enough and a squab dinner will make a meal fit for a king. Stealthy equipment could permit multiple sorties for an ongoing source of protein. Airguns tend to be very quiet - a useful advantage if low-impact hunting is necessary. Unin-formed people will lump them all together as simple BB guns, but some of today's airguns are incredible examples of precise manufacturing with astonishing capabilities. The general lack of knowledge does pro-vide a benefit. An airgun tends to be publicly more acceptable in areas that would raise firearm concerns.

It's an airgun and a very quiet one at that. Squab anyone?

The capabilities and limitations of these useful air-powered guns are best understood only after an in-depth look. That is the purpose of this book, the fourth of several "Survival Guns" firearm publications.

SURVIVAL GUNS: A BEGINNER'S GUIDE

In the first publication, we laid out some groundwork for a practical collection of firearms, and chosen from key requirements. Widespread use, dependability, ease of operation, availability of parts, acces-sories, and ammunition were thrown in the mix. Also covered was a hard look at firearms safety and responsible firearms ownership. Part of that process involved secure storage methods. We procured a gun safe and then framed up a small but practical inventory of firearms based on these require-ments, adding a shotgun, rimfire rifle, centerfire rifle, and a handgun. The idea was to choose, when possible, types with similar function. Use of each would thus promote skills with another to improve overall proficiency. Towards that goal, our initial selections were based on the Keep It Simple Stupid (K.I.S.S.) principle. We had to start *somewhere,* and most of us don't have deep enough pockets to rush headlong into the nearest Guns-R-Us for an armload of shootin' irons. We need something to cover the basics while saving for other items. That's where the next book begins...

SHOTGUNS: A COMPREHENSIVE GUIDE

The second edition serves as a specific starting point for a working gun battery, and thoroughly examines this versatile but often misunderstood firearm. The term "scattergun" is sometimes used to describe a multiple-projectile firearm with close range limitations. In actuality, a shotgun's pellet distribution is based on a number of factors, which can be regulated by knowledgeable shooters. It can also fire single projectiles to greatly extend its effective range or tackle the largest game. Once fully understood, the shotgun covers nearly all bases very well without a significant cash outlay. As a formidable defensive weapon and effective hunting tool, it makes a logical first choice for a surviv-al-oriented gun safe. The right shotgun can also serve nicely as a solid foundation for future acquisi-tions, which leads us to the third edition...

RIMFIRE RIFLES: A BUYER'S AND SHOOTER'S GUIDE

While a shotgun can cover many bases, a rimfire rifle can address a few special needs. The venerable "twenty-two" is often held in low regard, but raw power alone does not always constitute our best option. Especially in some survival circumstances, prudence may dictate an unobtrusive presence. The right rimfire choice can permit clandestine harvesting of small game or the elimination of pests. An array of highly interesting cartridges, from nasty high-speed loads to ultra-quiet rounds, provide this versatility. More potent rimfire options like the .17 caliber variants or .22 Magnum can effectively handle larger animals. In a pinch, all may even serve for self-defense. An economical .22 LR firearm can also serve as a great high-powered rifle trainer if similar function is considered. A rimfire can't do everything, but it can do a lot once fully understood. That's what this book is all about.

SELECTION GUIDELINES

Let's examine the key requirements referenced in the previous editions. With apologies to those readers who already labored through them, the criteria may avoid future headaches.

➤ **Whatever we're looking at must be in widespread use:** In the case of an airgun, we could substitute "must" for "should". If a primary firearm breaks, we're vulnerable until repairs can be made. If an airgun quits, it may not be as big a crisis. Still, an established and widely distributed design is reassuring.

➤ **Whatever we choose should be something with a solid reputation for dependability**: It's comforting to have confidence in a chosen tool. As explained in *Survival Guns*, there are teething pains with many new products, and guns are no exception.

➤ **It must be easy to operate:** If time and range access are issues, simple is better. Since we may be using an airgun as a trainer for other systems, it's worth thinking on a larger scale. Also, simpler designs normally offer less opportunity for breakage. But even the simplest systems can quit working at some point, so…

➤ **Parts must be readily available:** The Remington Model 870 shotgun has been in continuous production since 1950, with more than 10 million produced. In other words, plenty of spare parts are in circulation. The same cannot be said of most airguns, which occupy a niche market. Still, we may need access to servicing or parts, meaning an obscure brand could pose problems.

➤ **Ammunition must be widely available:** The .22 Long Rifle is a universal load, unlike the recent but obscure .17 Mach 2. The same logic applies to airgun pellets, .25 caliber types being harder to locate. However, unlike rimfire ammunition, which has undergone a recent scarcity, common caliber .177 and .22 airgun projectiles have remained readily available. Mainstream choices will just about always be cheaper, and if you're scrounging, the odds will tip in your favor.

➤ **It must be easy to maintain:** Airguns don't burn powder, and generally won't need disassembly. However, they *do* require lubrication. The spring-powered guns produce plenty of vibration, so occasional screw tightening can be necessary. Simpler designs facilitate the process, which will also prolong the life of your investment.

➤ **It should accommodate practical accessories:** Fortunately, when it comes to airguns, add-ons are less of a concern. One key item will likely be a scope, meaning that mounts need to be considered. Precharged airguns are often sold as repeaters, so extra magazines can be helpful. A sling may be in the soup as well. By sticking with the most popular guns, availability of such accessories is more likely.

➤ **It must represent good value:** The well-known rule of thumb is to buy the best equipment you can afford. However, "equipment" means more than just a gun. Some extras like a scope, mounts, sling, case, and ammo should be considered. The latest precharged rifles also need a high-pressure air source with fill connections. Adding up the essentials creates a figure constituting the real bottom line. We call this our "system cost". To stay within our means, some budgeting may be required, so an honest gun at a fair price helps keep a lid on costs.

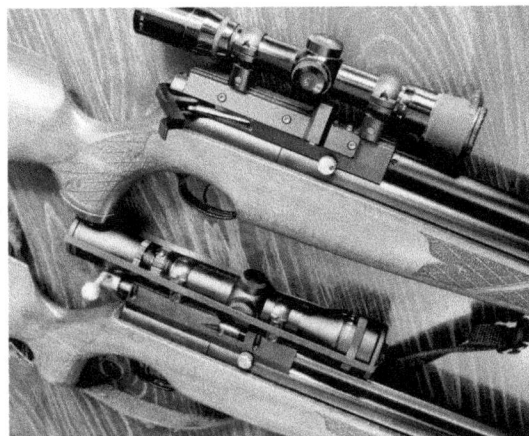

British high-performance airgun technology, not available in most big-box stores.

THE WRINKLE

When it comes to firearms, there are plenty of great choices. Airguns are a horse of a different color. Many gun stores and some big box retailers will have *something* in stock, but the most commonly seen airguns won't necessarily be your best bet. In fact, some of them are poorly engineered, with grossly overinflated performance figures. A basic understanding of the various power plants is a good first step in the purchasing process. From there, by keeping the above principles in mind, we can narrow down the field and shake out a practical choice without breaking the bank.

TABLE OF CONTENTS

ADDENDUM:

CHAPTER **1**

INTRODUCTION

Some firearms, like combination rifle/shotguns, could be viewed as specialty choices due to their unique designs and capabilities. By comparison, airguns occupy a completely unique niche. To the uninitiated, the term "airgun" often equates to a BB gun, which is associated with at least one blind eye. But there is another intriguing side to air-powered technology, which is far from a modern concept.

From a historical perspective, airguns are especially interesting. Some readers may be aware of the Girandoni pneumatic rifle used during the Lewis and Clark expedition more than two centuries ago. It was a large magazine-fed, 20-shot repeater that expelled .46 caliber lead balls from a high-pressure air flask, which doubled as its stock. Recharging the air reservoir was accomplished by use of a special hand pump that required more than a thousand strokes. During that era, projectiles were more commonly fired by caustic black powder, ignited by sparks from a flint. A shot produced a large volume of white, sulfurous smoke, followed by a laborious reloading process, which meant that repeating guns were almost unheard of. As such, an airgun demonstration involving multiple shots, without any telltale smoke, must have absolutely dazzled the Indians. They may very well have been kept at bay by the thought of such a weapon, which was, no doubt, the demonstration's purpose. In Europe, Napoleon's troops ran afoul of Austrian sharpshooters equipped with similar pneumatic arms. They posed a serious enough threat that Napoleon ordered the summary execution of any soldiers captured with such an arm. British gentry of the 19th century were especially fond of their air-powered "walking sticks", which were actually single-shot weapons disguised as canes.

This old Gat single-shot spring pistol is about as basic as an airgun can get. Its smoothbore breech-loading barrel will shoot just about any sort of .177 caliber projectile.

As firearms evolved, firepower increased, relegating airguns to small caliber recreational use. The ever-popular smoothbore BB gun has been a rite of passage for new shooters well in excess of a century. So-called "pellet guns" were rifled alternatives that shot low-powered .177 or .22 caliber lead projectiles for short-range shooting without noise or recoil. An obscure .25 caliber variant persisted, although it survived primarily abroad.

The Air Force pre-charged guns are the flip-side of air-powered technology. They're available in a number of calibers, right up to .45!

More recently big bore airguns have reappeared, thanks largely to the increasingly popular but modernized pre-charged technology used by Lewis and Clark. CNC manufacturing and refinements to the system have resulted in an affordable class of high-performance air rifles, capable of many useful shots from a single charge of air. It was only a matter of time until dedicated airgun aficionados realized that calibers beyond the classic .177 and .22 versions were feasible. The .25 returned, and is no longer uncommon. New .30 caliber offerings are gaining, and airguns can be purchased in .35, .45, and even .50 caliber.

Ballistic performance with .35 and .45 air rifles is on par with pistol cartridges of similar calibers. While few will dispute the defensive capabilities of a .45 caliber bullet, a few airgun issues complicate matters. First, achieving similar ballistics requires a relatively large volume of air, which typically reduces the number of practical shots to single digits. Secondly, good luck finding "pellets" if things go to hell. Also, these guns are quite a bit noisier than their small-bore .22 or .25 counterparts. Such concerns have not prevented some big bore airgun purists from using them on larger game. In fact, enough interest has developed to spark legislation in several states, permitting their use on species like

This .35 pellet is a mail-order proposition, whereas .22-caliber types remain a fairly common commodity.

hogs and whitetail deer. Use of smaller caliber, conventional airguns has long been legal in many jurisdictions for pests or game, like squirrels and rabbits.

While it's clear that the technology has matured, the use of airguns for defense remains sketchy. The larger caliber types may have enough punch, but their shot count is limited and also dependent on some sort of recharging process. Hunting larger game remains a possibility, since most such outings seldom requires more than a very few shots. But again, from an apocalyptic point of view, obtaining large caliber airgun projectiles seems iffy at best. It just might make more sense to stick with a conventional firearm that can also cover defensive needs.

However, there are other useful things we can do with an airgun. First off, we can shoot quietly and in limited spaces that would be off-limits to firearms. Not only that, but we can do so while undergoing less onerous legal restrictions. We can also more safely train new shooters, sharpen up our shooting eye, and hunt smaller critters. In general, we can accomplish these things for much less money if the right airgun choices are made.

One big plus is that BATF doesn't regulate airguns. Some states and municipalities do, but not the Feds. As a result, some airgun configurations that would require special licensing under National Firearms Act (NFA) guidelines don't apply. Short-barreled rifles of less than 16 inches normally need a special federal firearms stamp. With airguns, this restriction is off the table, explaining convertible pistol-to-rifle models. In many areas, these attributes may be an advantage, serving as a ticket into touchy places which would otherwise raise firearm concerns. We can also mail-order airguns and their projectiles without any federal constraints. Again, several states do regulate airguns, so any prospective buyer should first check their laws.

Because of ready firearms access here in America, the entire airgun field has got to be the least understood of all the shooting systems. Meanwhile, in more restrictive countries, firearms have become so highly regulated that they have been largely supplanted by airguns. Britain is a prime example, although even airgun ownership there involves power limits. The UK consumer market is thus oriented towards mid-powered airguns, some of which are exquisite examples of the gunsmith's art. Higher-powered versions are offered for those willing to undergo an arduous licensing process, but most such airguns are manufactured for export to the USA. In parts of Asia, the airgun rules are more lenient, while firearms are taboo. The result has been an explosion of new designs in a few really unusual big bore guns capable of taking deer-sized game.

These airguns have trickled into the United States, but most Americans still equate airguns with low-priced BB guns. Others have seen somewhat more sophisticated pellet guns advertised by big box sporting chains. However, there is yet another layer of advanced air-powered artistry. A nearly silent rifle built from blued steel and fine walnut is but one option. How about a .22 caliber air rifle you fill with a scuba tank? Maybe you'd like a .25 caliber version capable of killing raccoons. No problem; the sky's the limit. Tying these guns to survival use, clandestine hunting comes to mind. In that case, something quiet with adequate power is called for. Since it should not be dependent on hard-to-find necessities, an understanding of the basic power plants will be helpful.

If you view a rimfire rifle as an opportunity to improve or maintain centerfire skills, you may wish to consider an airgun in the same light. As a bolt-action fan, I've chosen hard-hitting centerfire rifles, .22 LR counterparts, and airguns that are all similarly configured. Targets and distances are simply

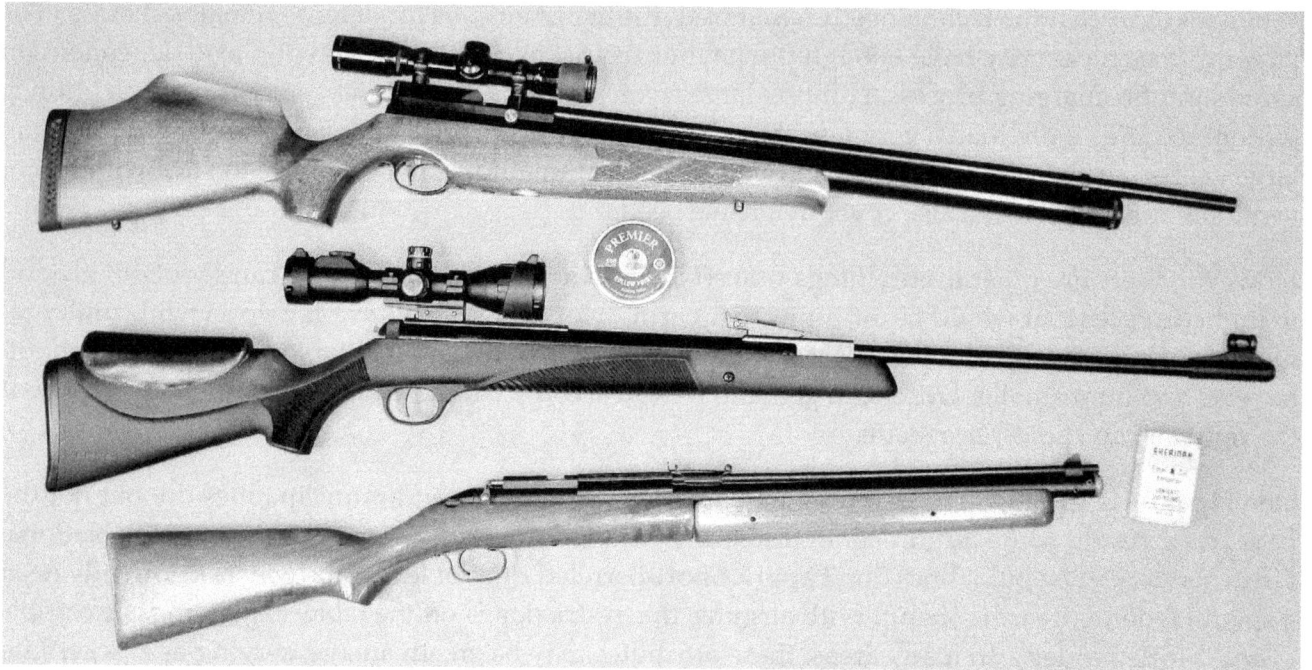

Three potential airgun systems include (top to bottom) a pre-charged pneumatic; barrel-cocking springer; and a pump-up pneumatic.

scaled to match their capabilities. In the case of the airguns, much of the shooting occurs right in the backyard. Owing to their nearly silent report, no one knows the difference.

Some less fortunate folks will get an automatic visit from their local SWAT team if *anything* resembling a firearm is seen near their premises. In that case, an indoor airgun range might be an option. Unlike powder-burning firearms, no elaborate noise abatement, ventilation, or backstop system will be necessary. Depending on the power of your airgun a "range" may be as simple as large box packed full of rags inside a basement. Although eye protection should always be worn, hearing protection won't be necessary with many air gun types.

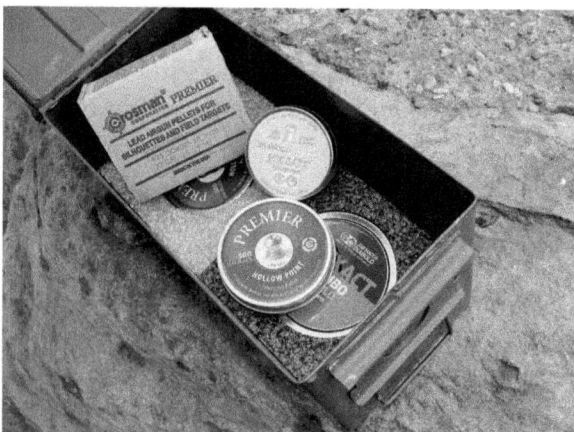

A surplus ammo can will hold thousands of pellets. Note the foam Pyramyd Air shipping protectors.

Despite a shortage of ammunition, airgun pellets can be found. Costs are still reasonable, and a tin of 500 of my favorite JSBs sells for less than $16. Once your gun is set up, few accessories will be necessary. A couple of 500-count pellet tins will last a fairly long time. Lacking any primer or powder, there's really nothing that can go bad beyond long-term pellet oxidation – something nearly any type of basic sealed container will take care of.

There is also one other huge dividend. An airgun will provide valuable extra practice, along with great entertainment, for very little long-term cost.

CHAPTER 2

A FIRST LOOK AT AIRGUNS

Airguns generally rely on four primary means to generate their power. In each instance, pressure is introduced to a barrel in order to expel a projectile. Typically, the gun will launch either a small spherical BB or a wasp-waisted pellet. In some designs, both types can be shot.

Another increasingly popular non-firearm type is an "Airsoft" gun. They often get lumped in with airguns, but differ in many respects. Most shoot plastic "BBs" of slightly larger diameter, at relatively low velocities of roughly 200 to 500 fps. Their primary uses involve informal close-range plinking and, in some cases, interactive force-on-force simulation. Many of the more sophisticated Airsoft guns bear a striking resemblance to their firearm counterparts, and share similar functions. Serious handgun competitors without ready range access sometimes set up indoor action-target courses to help maintain their skills. The guns typically run on cylinders of compressed gas or rechargeable batteries. Some even have full-auto capability, discharging a torrent of plastic balls. Accuracy is so-so due to smoothbore barrels, but the fun factor is real. Some readers may wish to further explore these guns for use as trainers. But for everyone in survival mode, a true airgun will be needed.

BB guns represent the next rung in power and the first step up the true airgun ladder. They use smoothbore barrels and shoot to Airsoft velocities of 300 to 600 fps, but the heavier steel projectiles hit considerably harder. A BB gun should never be discharged in the direction of a human or pet, and should be treated with the same respect as a firearm! That said, power and accuracy will be insufficient for ethical harvesting of species larger than sparrows at very close range.

Pellet guns shoot heavier but still relatively lightweight hourglass-shaped lead projectiles through rifled barrels, for greater accuracy. Some operate at BB gun velocities, making them strictly close-range affairs. Others develop considerably higher velocities, sufficient to harvest small game at distances of 40 yards or more.

Although it looks like a real Glock this air-soft pistol fires plastic 6mm spherical projectiles.

Common airgun projectiles include BBs, .177 and .22-caliber pellets.

Regardless of the type, all airguns expel their projectiles through some form of pressure. There are various ways to generate the requisite force, and each of the four popular systems is unique. In fact, the first may be debatable as an "air" gun at all.

CARBON DIOXIDE (CO2) POWERED GUNS

Most are lower-priced guns that rely on small disposable carbon dioxide cartridges that resemble miniature scuba tanks. Some others use larger refillable tanks. In either case, the principle remains the same. A small, metered volume of carbon dioxide is used to expel a projectile. Because it's a temperature-sensitive gas, CO2 has limits. Velocity is generally lower than the other systems, especially in colder weather. But once charged, you can just shoot away without much physical effort. For this reason, most repeaters run on CO2.

Typical CO-2 pellet pistol. This Daisy repeater shoots .177 pellets.

CO2 cartridge models: A popular example is a BB pistol, which can be inexpensively marketed due to the simplicity of feeding spherical projectiles. A supply of steel BBs is poured into the gun, which is then pressurized from a disposable CO2 cartridge manufactured for this purpose. Repeating pellet models typically work off small revolver-like rotating cylinders that feed .177 caliber lead projectiles. They may superficially resemble real semi-automatic pistols, but internally, they're revolvers. The true CO2 revolver knock-offs use the same technology. In either case, a CO2 cartridge is housed in the grip, providing somewhere around 40 to 60 shots. Velocity will usually run a modest 350 to 450 fps.

Some CO2 rifles are also sold. A few even run off a pair of disposable cartridges. Velocity will be higher than the handguns, but not as fast as their higher-pressure air-powered counterparts. Still, CO2 rifle velocity improves compared to the pistols, achieving 600 fps or a bit more with heavier .22 caliber pellets.

A disposable steel 12 gram CO-2 cartridge provides pressure and plastic pellet magazines are inserted from above.

Bulk-filled guns: A few CO2 rifles operate like paintball guns, running off a larger-volume onboard tank which may or may not be detachable. These guns require a CO2 fill station, which many paintball vendors maintain. Lots more shooting is possible, but of course, refills aren't as simple. Velocity remains similar, in the 600 fps range. One clever new rifle is the dual-fuel "Discovery", which can also run on high-pressure air at much greater velocity. More on that shortly…

<u>CO2 advantages:</u> No real physical exertion is required, and once pressurized, quick repeat shots are possible. Propellant gas can also be harnessed to cycle the actions of semi-automatic guns for high-volume plinking within the limits of the CO2 source.

<u>CO2 disadvantages:</u> Dependence on an external source of pressure is necessary, although a large but non-portable industrial CO2 tank will service bulk-filled guns for a very long time. The gas source will impose additional cost. It is also temperature-sensitive, producing lower velocity in colder weather. Many manufacturers will advise shooting these guns until their pressure is completely exhausted, which helps maintain seal life. Nevertheless, eventual leakage is a common malady. Those using CO2 cartridges should keep a good stash on hand.

SPRING GUNS

With this design, a spring-powered piston is driven forward inside a steel cylinder. Air pressure rapidly develops in front of the piston head and is forced through a small transfer port behind the barrel. It's the blast of air, and not the actual spring, that expels the projectile. Some means to retract and capture the piston/spring assembly is necessary, but this process is a one-stroke motion.

The piston of a spring gun is driven forward to rapidly compress air and expel a projectile.

The most familiar spring gun is probably an inexpensive smoothbore BB gun like Daisy's Red Ryder, which has been around for decades. Cocking is accomplished by cycling a lever, and a large supply of BBs is fed by gravity from an internal supply. In Europe and the UK, onerous firearms restrictions resulted in the refinement of this principle. A whole series of well-built spring-powered guns evolved that were designed for adult marksmanship. A finely-rifled barrel permitted good accuracy with lead pellets, and additional power was achieved with beefed up parts.

Daisy's immortal Red Ryder BB gun embodies the American perception of an airgun but times have changed.

It was only a matter of time before American shooters took notice. Robert Beeman probably did more than anyone to introduce quality springers by importing well-built German guns, starting back in the 1970s. The timing meshed with more restrictive firearm laws and shooters seeking practical alternatives. The adult airgun market grew, and spring-powered types moved to the mainstream.

Standard spring designs: Lately, the U.S. is awash with fairly inexpensive imports, most of which are barrel-cockers. The barrel is hinged to the front of the compression cylinder and is connected to the piston by a steel linkage. Drawing the barrel downward from the muzzle end applies the requisite force to cock the gun, and exposes the breech end for loading. On the barrel's full downstroke, the linkage passes through a long forend slot to provide the necessary clearance. The slot rules out attachment of a front sling stud or bipod.

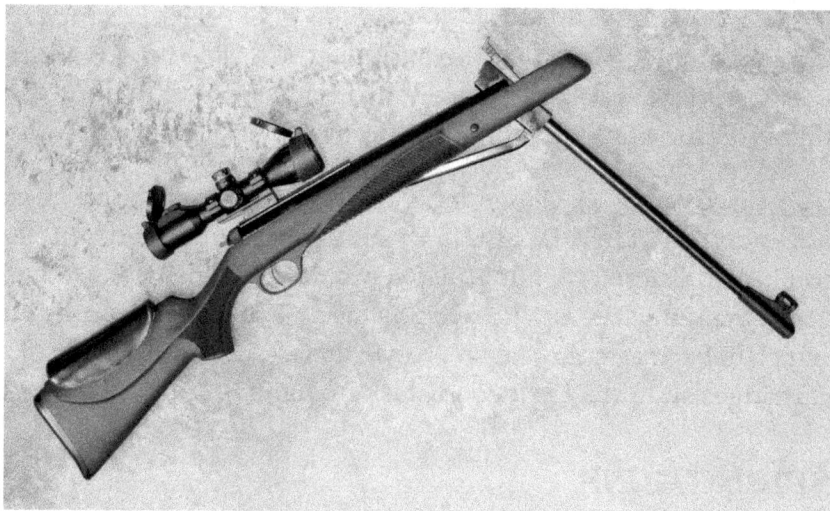

Typical barrel-cocking springer. Note the connecting linkage driven by the barrel.

Alternate versions use a sidelever or underlever in lieu of the barrel. Two such RWS examples are the Model 48 and Model 460. Both are large and potent spring rifles with fixed barrels: designs which should theoretically improve accuracy. Higher velocity comes with a price, and a more powerful gun will require more cocking force. The full effort will often be listed in pounds, running from perhaps 20 up to 40 or more. The higher-poundage rifles are really stout, but you'll only need one stroke to ready a spring gun for discharge. Each shot requires a separate cocking and loading process, so sustained shooting can be tiring. Repeating models aren't really practical, due to the inherent design of a springer.

The majority of springers shoot .177 pellets, with .22 versions coming in second. A few guns are also sold in .20 and .25 caliber. Some of these rifles can generate decent power thanks to a heavy spring and large compression tube. For whatever reason, in many cases the listed velocities seem to

An under-lever springer with a fixed barrel, which in theory, should be a bit more accurate.

be "optimistic". The highest advertised velocities run well over 1100 fps in .177, but extremely light, non-lead pellets are used to stretch the speed. Don't be shocked if your gun is slower. In the real world, a 950 fps .177 is a speedy pellet rifle, as is a 750 fps .22. Sure, there are rifles that do better, but not as many as advertising indicates. More power comes from stiffer springs and larger pistons, resulting in a very heavy gun.

Spring-powered pistols are also sold, but velocity will be much less and more in line with the CO2 type guns. Most lack enough size for a potent powerplant and those with greater velocity are very large. At some point it just makes more sense to carry a mid-powered and compact rifle.

Gas piston (or gas ram) guns: Instead of a powerful coil spring, the main cylinder is sealed to contain a charge of inert gas (or sometimes air), which is compressed by the piston during cocking. The principle is similar to a gas strut or heavy-duty vehicle shock absorber. Air rifles using this design produce less vibration and don't suffer in velocity. One big advantage of a gas piston gun is that you can leave it cocked. That's not recommended with spring models, which can gradually lose power as the spring takes a set. Initially, gas ram designs were a novelty, but lately, they are becoming much more popular.

Spring and gas ram advantages: Operation is straightforward and the power source is self-contained, eliminating worries about CO2 cartridges, pumps, or scuba tanks. Useful accuracy and power can be acquired with careful shopping, and the guns tend to be a bit quieter than other types. You can just pick one up and shoot it whenever you wish. Most of these guns are also fully ambidextrous - something lefties should consider.

Disadvantages: Guns with higher velocities will require considerable cocking effort. Some users may encounter difficulties, and extended shooting sessions will probably be tiring for all shooters. The sudden release of piston mass generates substantial reverse recoil. Special airgun-rated scopes are needed to prevent their quick destruction, along with slip-proof mounts. Hold sensitivity is a product of these dynamics, and mastery of correct shooter technique is necessary to overcome erratic shots. A bipod won't solve the problem, and is impractical with barrel-cocking rifles. Shooting from prone is also difficult. A spring gun should not remain cocked for too long a period. Gas ram models overcome this problem, but special high-flashpoint lubricants will be needed with either type (although cost is not a major issue).

MULTI-PUMP (OR PUMP-UP) PNEUMATICS

Pump-up airguns are nothing new, relying on a succession of strokes from a built-in mechanism that gradually develops a charge of air. More strokes equal more pressure (to a point), and velocity can be regulated by the number of pumps: usually 8 to 10. Squeezing the trigger releases a spring-powered striker that knocks a valve open. All of the pressure is then released into the barrel, where it forcefully expels the projectile. The entire process is repeated for each new shot, making this system physically demanding.

Compared to a spring gun of similar velocity, the instant depressurization of a pneumatic tends to be louder. A pump-up rifle will also be more difficult to scope, because one of the shooter's hands needs

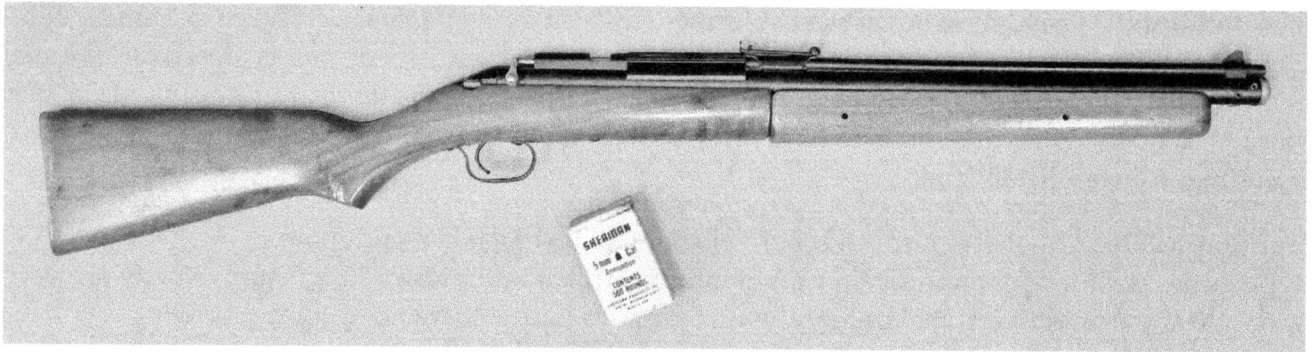

The Sheridan 5mm is a classic pump-up pneumatic airgun.

to grasp the receiver for best pumping leverage. In the 1960s, wood-stocked Benjamin and Crosman single-shot rifles were popular pellet guns, offered in .177 and .22 models. A similar well-built Sheridan pump-up rifle was available in a novel (for that time) 5mm (.20 caliber), which shot a conical bullet-like projectile. The guns all worked in a similar manner, with a hinged forend pumping arm and a small bolt that cocked an internal valve striker. As plastics evolved, repeating BB models appeared, feeding from an internal reservoir. Single .177 pellets could be singly loaded, but regardless of the choice, they still needed re-pumping between each shot. Power was roughly in line with CO_2 rifles, and both types often shared many main parts. Velocity with a .22 or .20 was in the 600 fps range, with .177 calibers doing a bit better. Pump-up pistols were also popular plinkers, producing less power and noise. Similar versions of these guns continue to be produced.

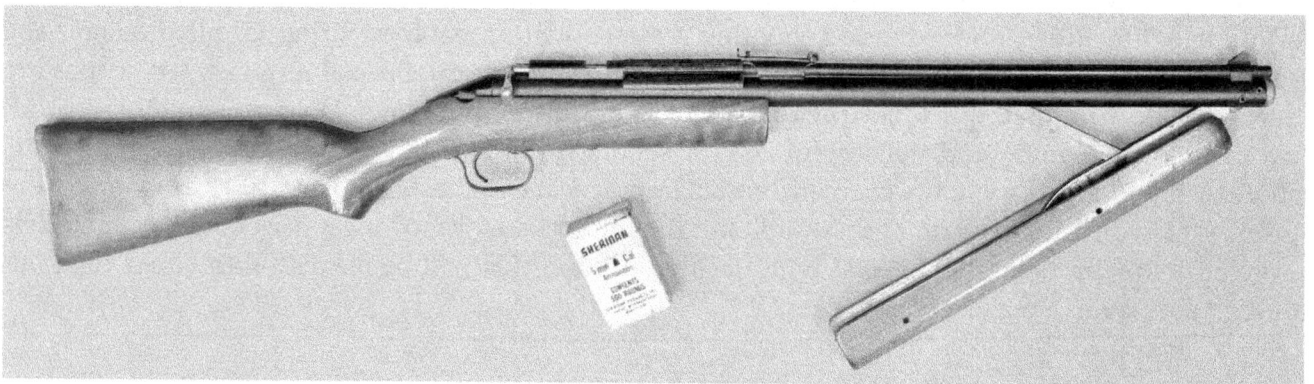

The Sheridan's hinged forearm is used to develop a charge of air through multiple strokes.

<u>Pump-up advantages:</u> The pump-up pneumatic provides a self-contained system in a fairly lightweight package. With a modicum of care, it will probably last for decades. An occasional drop of 30 weight motor oil on the seals and each pivot point should keep one running. Power can be regulated by the number of pump strokes, and four or five will suffice for close-range plinking with a little less noise. A pneumatic can remain pressurized, and most have a safety button. You can pump one up, load it, and sneak around the puckerbrush. For a little more safety, it can remain pressurized but unloaded. Recoil is nil, so no special scope is needed - assuming you can figure out a practical way to mount one.

Disadvantages: Velocity will be less than the so-called "magnum" springers, but the report will be louder, with an audible "snap!" The actual pumping process is also fairly noisy, since during each stroke, the forend loudly contacts the metal pressure tube. This process can be quite tiring during prolonged shooting sessions. Just about everyone will be tempted to exceed the maximum number of pumps, but more force is necessary for each stroke, which is hard on the gun. This will result in little gain and the air reservoir will become "air locked". In this situation, its internal pressure will exceed the striker's ability to knock the valve open, rendering the system inoperable. For those with good eyes, the issued open sights may be adequate for close-range use. For others, although clamp-on scope mounts are available, optics remain problematic. So does the attachment of a sling.

SINGLE-STROKE PNEUMATICS

This design is similar to the multi-pumps, the main difference being that full pressure is developed from just one stroke. Many single-stroke types are highly accurate target guns, designed for official 10-meter competition. They shoot match grade .177 pellets into very tiny groups, thanks to a vibration-free system with consistent pressure. A few models are intended for junior clubs, but many are Olympic-grade guns that cost serious money. Accuracy is paramount and high velocity isn't needed. For rifles or pistols, most single-strokes shoot below 600 fps, which is the optimum velocity for best accuracy with match pellets. They are often charged from a long side lever that requires minimal effort.

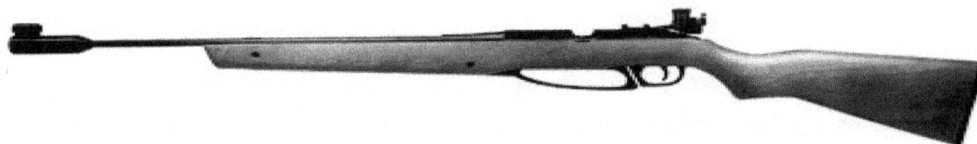

Daisy's Avanti is a single-stroke pneumatic air rifle often used by junior target club shooters.

Single-stroke advantages: The lower velocity requires less cocking effort. Vibration and recoil is non-existent, as is hold sensitivity. Accuracy can be phenomenal, and the higher-end guns are true precision masterpieces.

Disadvantages: In most instances, you can swing the charging arm to your heart's content with no increase in power. The tiny pellets at sedate velocities lack useful punch for any survival-type use. So from now on, the single-stroke design is out of the running.

PRE-CHARGED (OR PRE-COMPRESSED) PNEUMATICS

These guns are similar to pump-up or single-stroke guns, but they are charged from an external high-pressure air source. On most PCP designs, the air is stored in a tubular steel reservoir located under the barrel. A few rear-mounted paintball-type stock systems are also employed.

Most folks fill their PCP guns from a scuba tank, to around 2800 - 3,000 psi. That's some serious pressure, which you'll never achieve with a bicycle pump. However, a similar but highly specialized high-pressure air pump is sold, which takes the place of a tank. It takes a huge amount of effort to fully charge the gun, which accounts for the popularity of scuba systems.

Like the pump-up guns, PCP rifles are loud. Most are also much more expensive; however, many now have built-in "sound moderators" that greatly reduce their report. The barrel is surrounded by an external sleeve that extends beyond the muzzle. This shroud may also have a few relief ports to help dissipate pressure. Instead of a very audible crack, the report is reduced to that of a gas-powered nail gun (or even lower).

The number of shots available from one charge of air is dependent on several factors, including the gun's reservoir's capacity. Somewhere between 25 to 45 shots is a reasonable expectation before pressure subsides and reduces velocity. At that point, you can hook the gun up to an HPA hose, and fill it from the air source of your choice. Repeating PCP guns are now fairly common, and many are bolt-actions that run off small revolving magazines.

A pair of high-end PCP rifles that run off different reservoirs. The Air Arms has a fixed pressure tube and the BSA employs a removable bottle.

PCP advantages: Once charged with air, repeat shots are nearly effortless, requiring only the cycling of a bolt or other cocking mechanism that makes repeating guns practical. High-pressure air permits high velocity, which serves to flatten out trajectory while increasing terminal energy. The same pressure also generates more useful speed for larger pellets such as .25 caliber (or bigger) projectiles. PCP guns can remain charged indefinitely, and most (but not all) have a safety. For field use, such guns can be carried, ready for use, in a manner similar to firearms. Recoil is nil, so special airgun scopes are not necessary. Sound moderators are increasingly common, resulting in some of the most silent airguns on the market.

Disadvantages: Air is free, but the high pressure required to power a PCP gun requires an external source of some type. A scuba tank will support hundreds of shots (from multiple gun refills), but it will eventually need a dive shop recharge. Whether steel or aluminum, it will also be impractical to lug around, although small and lighter carbon fiber versions are available. Some are rated for extra pressure, but may exceed compressor capabilities. All require periodic inspections, too. Dedicated airgun compressors can be purchased for substantial additional cost, but none of these systems are truly portable. A special PCP hand pump can do the job for those willing to expend the effort. An initial air charge may require hundreds of strokes, and from that point, you may need roughly two pumps per shot to replenish the gun's capacity. Although the better pumps include a filter and moisture trap, internal gun corrosion remains a concern. Safe containment of high-pressure air is serious business, which also requires meticulous engineering. PCP gun prices generally run higher, and the fill accessories greatly increase system cost. A PCP gun will also need periodic maintenance for inspection of the air reservoir and replacement of seals. Higher-powered guns are quite loud if not moderated. Attachment of an accessory device may violate some restrictions.

AIR PISTOL COMMENTS

Unless you're looking strictly for a trainer, I'd skip an air pistol. Most just don't develop enough power to be useful in the field – especially for survival purposes. Some are on the edge, but they are just plain big. The PCP pistols have more oomph, but the smaller pistols lack practical air capacity. Overall, I'd rather tote a rifle. It will generally be more convenient to carry, and will also be a whole lot easier to shoot. One possible exception is Benjamin's U.S.-built "Marauder" PCP pistol. It puts out useful power, developing around 700 fps with a standard weight .22 caliber pellet. The barrel has a sound-moderating shroud and is fed from a bolt-activated 8-shot magazine. The gun is large, but not overly heavy. Its best attribute – an accessory shoulder stock - actually removes it from true pistol classification. Once installed, you gain a lightweight, NFA legal short-barreled carbine. We'll take a closer look at this gun further on…

Chapter 3

AIRGUN PROJECTILES

The typical choices for years have boiled down to spherical steel BBs or wasp-waisted "diabolo" projectiles. Most of the latter have domed heads and hollow skirts. Air pressure expands the soft lead skirt to seal the bore, and the shape is designed to minimize barrel friction. Other nose shapes include pointed, hollow-point, or flat point "wadcutter" profiles. None are particularly aerodynamic, and all are designed for subsonic stability. Lately, some unorthodox designs have emerged with lead bodies and plastic tips, plastic skirts with steel heads, or light alloy construction.

While BB guns are fun, they have little to offer here. Most are low-velocity smoothbores with mediocre accuracy and poor killing power. Still, we'll include them in the list of common projectiles:

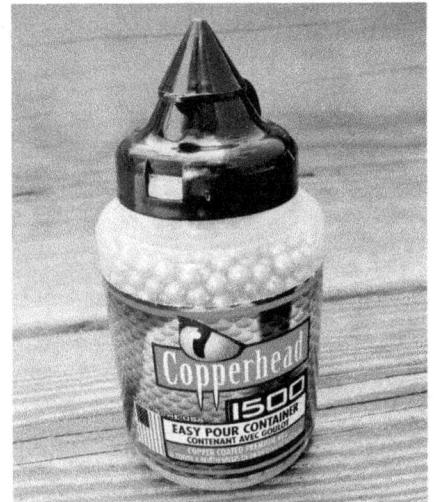

This container of BBs represents a whole lot of inexpensive shooting.

Steel BBs on a magnetic tool. They'll ricochet off hard surfaces.

BB or airgun shot: The typical BB is a steel .172 caliber sphere which is usually zinc or copper-plated, for use in smoothbore guns. It will easily pass through a rifled .177 caliber pellet gun, and some manufacturers advertise their guns with this capability. In most instances, such types will be lower-priced domestic products intended for casual users. A steel BB is hard on a well-built rifled barrel, and could also roll out the muzzle. A gun designed for BBs will often have a magnetic retainer to hold it at the breech. So, shooting a BB through a true pellet gun could not only damage the bore, but also cause dry-fire damage to a springer. BBs will also ricochet like crazy off of hard surfaces. Shooting glasses are always advised, but with BBs they're essential. The average projectile weighs around 5 grains. A heavier but less common .177 lead "air rifle shot" is also sold for use in some repeating rifles.

Darts: I remember shooting these from a friend's pump-up .177 Benjamin pistol as a teenager. We probably didn't do its brass rifled barrel any favors. These projectiles really are miniature darts, with pointed tips, a cylindrical metal body, and a trailing skirt. They'll stick in soft targets at low velocity. They will also ricochet off hard surfaces. Darts should only be fired from smoothbore barrels. Better yet, just skip them entirely.

Cleaning pellets: We'll come back to these bore-diameter felt cylinders in the cleaning and maintenance chapter. Essentially, they're soft pellets that some folks shoot to clean their barrels.

Felt cleaning pellets and .177 airgun darts.

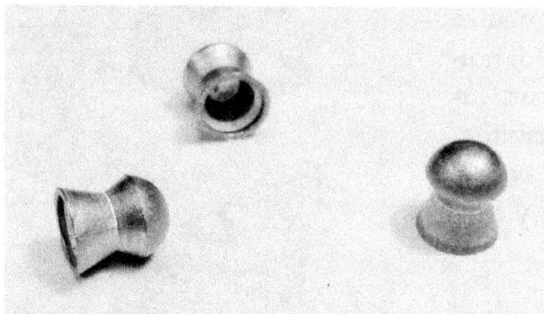

Typical diabolo-type domed pellets with hollow skirts. Their wasp waists minimize barrel friction, and produce a center-of-gravity similar to Badminton birdie.

.177 (or 4.5mm) pellet: The most common airgun caliber, it's popular around the world. Labeling will often indicate the European 4.5mm designation. Most true match type guns shoot .177 diabolo pellets, which are capable of excellent accuracy. Much of this shooting occurs indoors, where wind drift is not a concern. The pellets normally weigh somewhere between 7 and 10 grains, with a few field types pushing 16 grains. Outdoors, wind is a real concern. The heavier versions may offer a bit less drift, and will also hit a bit harder. The heaviest will start with less velocity and have a steeper trajectory. The fastest rifles can offset these disadvantages to some degree, but a .177 isn't really the best choice for use on species larger than starlings. For many adults, the tiny pellets are also difficult to load.

.20 (or 5mm): Sheridan popularized this caliber as the "5mm Sheridan Pellet", designed for their well-known pump-up rifle of the same name. The pellets were heavier than normal, with cylindrical bodies and a pointed tip. During the 1980s, diabolo designs appeared as a bridge between the .177 and .22 offerings. Beeman began promoting .20 caliber guns, advertising high-end springers geared towards field use. In any given rifle, velocity was a bit lower than a .177, but still faster than a .22. Trajectory fell in between, as did terminal effect. The caliber continues with some popularity, although not on the scale of its siblings. Most weigh between 10 and 14 grains, but choices are much more limited.

This array of airgun projectiles includes a steel BB plus .177; .20; .22; .25; and .35-caliber lead pellets. Note the different nose designs.

.22 (or 5.5mm): The second most common airgun caliber after the .177, it's just a larger version. Labeling of foreign brands may indicate 5.5mm. More recently, Gamo began offering non-lead .22 pellets, like their PBA. It only weighs 9.7 grains, permitting velocities as high as standard .177 types. The higher speed sells lots of guns, but performance fades quickly as range increases. Most .22 types weigh 12 to 18 grains, the majority being around 14 to 16 grains. You won't see too many true match guns in .22 caliber, but you will observe better punch on small critters. Accuracy can still be excellent, and the larger-diameter pellets are easier to handle. The selection is somewhat smaller than .177s, but still more than adequate.

.25 (or 6.35mm): Although this caliber has been around for many years, it has only recently gained popularity. Part of the push may be due to increases in air gun power, permitting velocities sufficient to flatten trajectory. Most weigh between 25 and 30 grains, a substantial increase over average .22 offerings. Some .25 projectiles exceed 40 grains, which is the .22 LR standard. However, velocity will be much less and trajectory will be greatly exaggerated. Guns will be either "magnum" springers or PCP rifles. Right now, there are probably more .25 choices than .20 caliber pellets.

Other calibers: For the true airgun specialists, some very interesting calibers have emerged. These include .30, .35, 45, and .50 caliber giants, which are usually expelled by compressed air. They're interesting options, to say the least! Most, but not all, are made in Korea. It takes quite a bit of air to launch big, heavy pellets, so shots per charge are limited. With only 5 to 7 available, a high-pressure air source needs to be somewhere close by. The .35 caliber produces power similar to a .380 pistol load. The .45 will perform similarly to a .45 ACP, and the .50 is pretty much in the same boat. With very careful shot placement, the latter calibers will anchor larger game. Since the "pellets" are for the most part just light, lead pistol bullets, headshots

This collection of airgun pellets represents a mere fraction of the many choices.

would be advised. These big bore guns are not firearms, and they don't emit a muzzle flash. However, the limitations imposed by air capacity and ammo are real concerns. Think you'll find any at your local hardware store? That's the problem.

CHOOSING A CALIBER

Most of us are better off sticking with the more popular choices, and when it comes to subsistence hunting, it might as well be a .22.

The .177, although the most common airgun bore, has noticeably less punch on live targets. The .20 offers perhaps marginal improvement, but suffers from fewer pellet choices and limited availability.

A .25 caliber will generally hit harder than its smaller brethren, assuming it travels at adequate velocity. However, this is often a problem for large bore spring guns, which suffer from energy loss and steeper trajectories. Many of the latest pre-charged .25 caliber guns can overcome these issues, but their users will be tethered to charging paraphernalia, normally at greater overall cost. Those interested in a .25 caliber airgun should lay in a large supply of pellets as a precautionary measure. In fact, regardless of the caliber, a generous supply of ammunition makes sense. Luckily, airgun pellets are all portable. Lots of .22 pellets will fit in a pill container, which will easily slip in a pocket. If separated from the main supply, the odds of locating this common caliber are greatly increased.

As for shapes, the pointed pellets are designed for penetration, but will cause little tissue damage. Some of the hollow-point designs may expand with bone contact, but you can't plan on it. They're really just domed pellets with a shallow cavity. I use good quality domed pellets for just about all uses, from targets to small game. The only exception involves the use of a .177 air rifle for pest birds up to pigeon size. In that case, I'll sacrifice aerodynamic qualities and range for a flatpoint wadcutter nose, to maximize impact force and tissue damage. In fact, at extremely close range, some airgunners go a step further by shooting pellets loaded backwards. It's strictly a close-range proposition, since accuracy will likely suffer. So far, I've refrained from trying this in any shrouded barrel airguns, for fear of a pellet striking a baffle or end cap.

When it comes to brands, I'm a fan of JSB Pellets, which are made in the Czech Republic. Accuracy has often been excellent, and different types are offered for all of the common calibers. You won't find them in the big box stores, but the online airgun dealers stock them. In higher velocity airguns, my favorite is the .22 JSB "Diabolo Exact Jumbo", which weighs 15.9 grains. The slightly lighter JSB 14.3 grain "Diabolo Jumbo Express" is another favorite in mid-powered guns. Crosman's "Premier Domed" 14.3 pellets often do well, too.

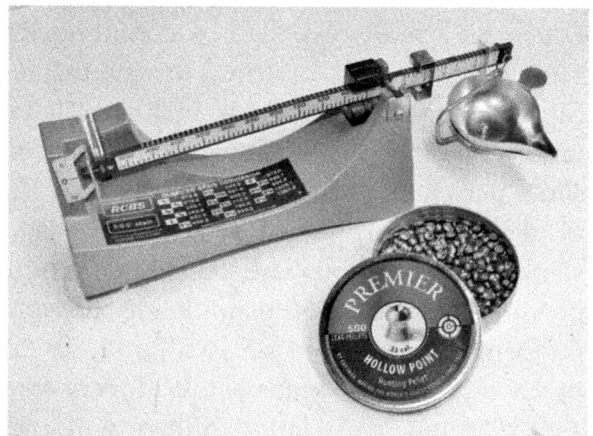

A reloading scale indicates this .22 pellet matches its advertised weight of 14.3 grains.

Unfortunately, there really isn't a universal top choice. The best bet is to carefully shoot a few types from your rifle and order the most accurate brand. You can pay less for cheaper pellets, but accuracy will really suffer. Even the better brands are fairly affordable.

CHAPTER 4

AIRGUN POWER, RANGE AND ACCURACY

First of all, we need to put everything into perspective. Even most of the so-called "magnum" air rifles are less powerful than A .22 Short. Sure, you'll see many .177 models advertised as 1000+ fps guns. Well, maybe, but you can bet that the lightest pellets were used. Even if close to reality, little 17 caliber projectiles weighing less than 9 grains may start off fast, but they just don't have much mass. Their velocity will quickly decrease, which limits penetration.

As for accuracy, each airgun system has its quirks. Ironically, the intrinsically most accurate type – the single-stroke pneumatic – lacks useable power for our purposes. Still, a practical level of accuracy is attainable from the other powerplants. We just need to understand the factors that influence on-target results.

POWER

When it comes to airguns, this is really a relative term. Overall, even compared to a bullet fired from a .22 rimfire, it's pretty limited. In my experience, a .177 is far less effective than a .22 caliber pellet, even if the latter begins its journey with 25% less velocity. You can kill squirrels and pigeons with a .177, but surgical shot placement is essential. The larger .22 pellets seem to hit noticeably harder, and are my preferred choice. This edited chart from *Rimfire Rifles: A Survival Guide* is an attempt to quantify the so-called killing power of these projectiles.

Small-bore Killing Power: With hits to upper-body areas and average ballistic performance.						
Caliber	Starling	Pigeon	Crow	Squirrel	Woodchuck	Fox
.177 Airgun	DRT	Recov	Marginal	Marginal	NEG	—
.22 Airgun	DRT	DRT	Recov	Recov	NEG	—
.22 LR HVHP	DRT	DRT	DRT	DRT	Marginal	Marginal
Codes DRT: *Dead right there.* NEG: *Not enough gun.* Recov: *Recoverable. Quarry may travel a short distance.*						

Disclaimer: The above information is based mostly on my own experience. In other words, it's not derived from empirical data. No doubt others will have varying opinions. Consider it as no more than a rough guide.

Note that the chart references hits to upper body areas like the heart and lungs. I know a guy who claims he killed a deer by shooting it in the eye at close range with a .20 caliber pump-up pellet rifle. That's not only highly unethical, but also illegal just about everywhere. But it does illustrate a point; hits to the central nervous system are different. Although not listed here, plenty of deer have been killed that way with .22 rifles, a good many after dark. On airgun-sized quarry, the brain is a very small target, although it's a spot worth trying for whenever reasonably possible. There is a very good chance that animals up to the size of a woodchuck will quickly

Yes, you can kill a woodchuck with a the right airgun, but precise pellet placement is necessary.

succumb from a headshot with all three guns on the list. However, even with a .22 LR hollow-point, an upper body shot could easily result in a groundhog escaping to its burrow. And as often as not, a body will be the easier and more common mark. So that's the criteria used above, as inexact as it is. More qualified people than me have labored over formulae capable of cataloging so-called stopping power. It's easier said than done!

Projectile energy: Examining the published ballistic data associated with conventional ammunition, we'll typically see a list of calibers, along with their bullet weights, muzzle velocities, and energy. The latter figure is expressed in foot-pounds, which are units of work for engineering or ballistic purposes. One pound of force applied through a displacement of one foot equals 1 ft·lb of energy. With projectiles, bullet weight and velocity produce the numbers. But foot-pounds can be deceiving. A .22 Long Rifle bullet might start out with 100 ft·lbs. of energy. However, a close range shot will not produce the same effect as getting hit by a 100-pound rock. In fact, the physical reaction probably won't even be close.

It would also be possible to fire two loads with identical projectile weights and velocities, but different bullet designs. While each would produce the same foot-pounds of energy, their terminal effects could vary greatly. Compared to a non-expanding round nose bullet, a mushrooming hollow-point will produce a larger wound channel. That's why it is such a popular hunting or defensive choice. It's also the reason I'm not too fixated on metallic cartridge foot-pound listings.

But airgun pellets work with less in both velocity and mass. They quickly shed velocity and are unlikely to display classic hollow-point expansion at most field distances. The HP types more often behave like typical domed pellets, so diameter (or caliber) becomes a better predictor of tissue destruction. Projectile weight and velocity create the foot-pound numbers we can use to compare impact force. That's why I pay more attention to airgun foot-pound numbers.

Granted, this is a greatly simplified explanation of the whole process, but it may help put things in perspective.

Pellets and foot-pounds: Again, to quantify power (what little there is), foot-pounds of energy make a good airgun barometer. Some fantastic rifles come out of the UK, where their legal limit is 12 ft·lbs. Anything more requires a hard-to-get Firearms Certificate (FAC). With a common 8 grain .177 pellet, that translates to a MV of around 825 fps. Switching to a .22, a slower but fairly standard 14.3 grain pellet with a MV of only 610 fps will also develop around 12 ft·lbs. The Brits kill plenty of vermin with that level of performance, so it certainly can be done. They hunt rabbits, pigeons, and other similar-sized pests, enjoying good success through very careful shooting and taking great care to aim at the very small spots needed to penetrate vital organs. It's probably no accident that some of the most accurate airguns are built in Great Britain.

The FAC-rated export versions of these British-built guns are capable of extra power. They are manufactured in other countries as well, including the United States. For humane hunting, a few extra foot-pounds help. We all strive for precise shot placement, but field conditions can often make this difficult. For good results on squirrels and pigeons, I look for a .22 pellet capable of achieving around 20 foot-pounds. I refer to these two species because they're good representative airgun targets, and also somewhat tenacious. To hit the 20 ft·lb level with a .22 airgun the same 14.3 grain pellet will need a MV of 800 fps. A .177 will need to hit 1060 fps with an 8 grain pellet.

It's no problem to reach 20 ft·lbs with a FAC-rated PCP rifle, but it can be problematic with some springers. That is, unless you have one with a really hefty powerplant. The tradeoff is that it will then be harder to cock and more cumbersome to tote. I wouldn't go to the bank on any velocity claims of 800 fps with a mid-sized .22 springer. There's a very good chance it won't hit 700 fps! In the same gun, a .177 will probably be 200 fps faster; producing a MV of more like 900 fps. These velocities will develop energy somewhere between the U.K. 12 ft·lb limit and my highly subjective 20 ft·lb preference. Such performance is really not a disaster, but it may call for shorter shots. Remember, these numbers are generated at the muzzle. Pellets have poor aerodynamic characteristics, and quickly shed their velocities. Downrange energies will suffer as well.

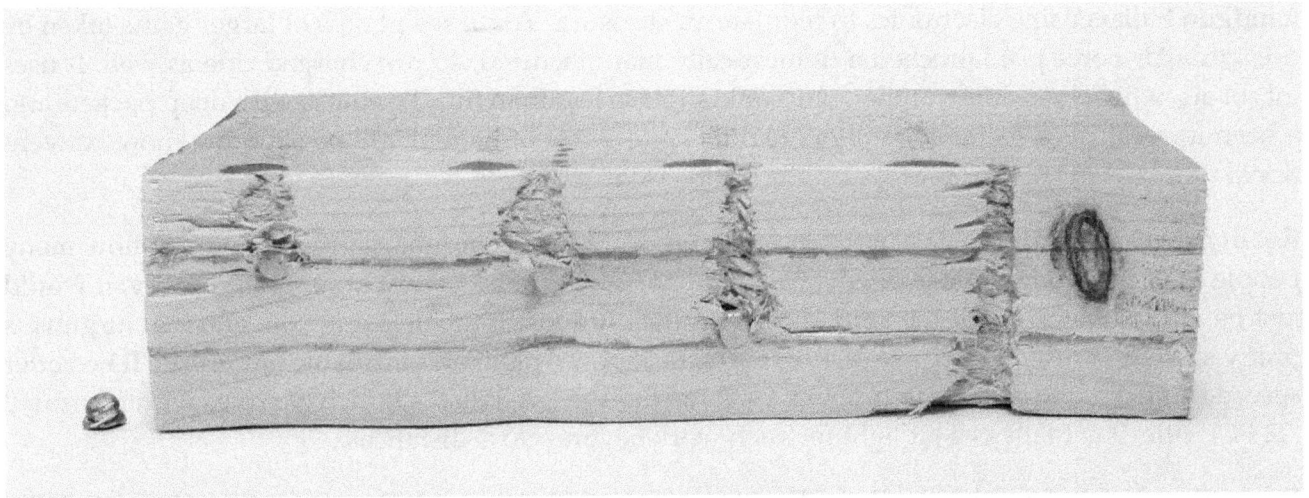

These .22 JSB 14.3 grain pellets were shot into a section of 2x4 from 10 yards at muzzle velocities of (L-R): 700 fps; 800 fps; and 900 fps. A 29 grain .22 Short fired at 950 fps passed through. Clearly, projectile mass counts. The lines are graduated in ½-inch increments and the deformed pellet was dug out of another section.

Other factors: Foot-pounds alone aren't the whole story. Even though hollow-point pellets are available, we really can't plan on reliable expansion. Compared to a .177 pellet, the frontal surface of a .22 causes much more tissue damage, hitting with an audible "smack". At 910 fps with a 16 grain pellet, my Air Arms PCP rifle develops nearly 30 foot-pounds of muzzle energy. That sounds impressive, and I'm happy with the gun. But to put things in perspective, a standard-velocity 29 grain .22 Short with a muzzle velocity of 1045 fps develops around 70 ft·lbs of muzzle energy.

Back in airgun land, a 20 ft·lb or greater pellet does provide some extra punch, but shot placement is still crucial. The explosive hydrostatic effects produced by high speed varmint bullets won't be seen. We're really just drilling a hole through tissue, so death is more a product of hemorrhaging than immediate shock. True, this effect is often evident on starling-sized birds, and those hit in the upper body by a .22 caliber, 20 foot-pound airgun will plummet with nary a quiver. Pigeons may often exhibit frenetic flapping, but will also quickly drop. On the other hand, larger birds like crows, as well as many furred species, may just soak up a pellet without instant results – especially at longer ranges.

Beeman Precision Airguns popularized .20 caliber rifles during the 1980s; the theory being that they offered the flatter trajectory of .177s and the punch of .22 pellets. Maybe, but you can't prove it by me. I owned a bunch of different springers in .20 caliber before returning to the larger .22. Lately, the .25 is gathering steam, and it seems like a good idea. With a bigger frontal area, a fast-stepping .25 caliber pellet should hit like Thor's hammer (relatively speaking). Energy can approach 40 foot-pounds, so it would be my pick for animals up to the size of raccoons – assuming pellets were available. Strictly from a survivalist point of view, the .20 and .25 should probably be avoided. Either caliber is readily available online, but that won't help you much in a national fiasco.

Big bore pellets: The guns in .357, .45, or .50 caliber are an entirely different animal. Because the "pellets" are actually pistol bullets, I have no doubt a hog could be anchored by a well-placed slug traveling at .45 ACP velocities. For the lowdown on such guns, check out the Quackenbush website. It's interesting stuff! The Crosman website has a link to their Benjamin Rogue, which shoots lead .357 handgun bullets using electronics to regulate air pressure. You'll see photos of larger game taken by this gun. Air Force just launched a domestically manufactured .45 pre-charged rifle as well. It uses lots of air, which limits the number of useable shots to less than five. For those with deep pockets and a keen interest, such technology offers real intrigue. Most of us will still be shooting more conventional numbers in .177 or .22 caliber.

Reality check: Meanwhile, take another look at those .22 Short numbers and ask yourself how many people are going to hunt hogs or coyotes with one? It would be a stunt at best, but mostly, it would just be inhumane. Some of the stuff shown on the outdoor channels using conventional airguns is pretty sketchy. Within our parameters of a practical powerplant and available ammo, we'll be better served by sticking to cottontails or grackles. Even though I've killed a bunch of crows with my trusty .22 PCP rifle, it actually is a bit light for such work beyond close distances.

Power thresholds: I previously pitched a .22 airgun as the best overall choice, factoring in availability of pellets and terminal effects. Velocity will be the key to the latter consideration. In some cases, temperature can play a role. Revisiting the previous information, here are some guidelines:

<u>600 fps range:</u> For our purposes, this velocity will be our rock-bottom minimum. In .177, it's anemic but adequate for very small species at close range. You could expect to dine on a mourning dove hit with a flat point H&N Match pellet inside 20 yards. A .22 pellet will hit noticeably harder, upping the ante to pigeons, squirrels, or rabbits at the same range. The latter two should be taken with head shots if possible. Each primary airgun type (including CO_2 rifles) can reach this speed in .177 versions, and many can do so in .22 caliber. Don't forget that colder temperatures lower CO_2 pressure and velocity.

<u>700 fps range:</u> I'd want a .22 airgun approaching 700 feet per second with 14.3 grain pellets, which equals 15.5 ft·lbs. This is a stretch for the pump-up pneumatics, but most PCP rifles can easily break that speed. Some, but not all springers can achieve this performance, but again, the advertised numbers may be overly optimistic. Many 800 fps rifles are hard-pressed to reach 700 fps with standard weight .22 pellets. Less velocity equals steeper trajectory, which makes further hits more difficult. The vital zones of airgun-capable species are fairly small, so precise shooting is necessary. A velocity in the 700 fps range will effectively work on squirrel-sized targets out to 30 yards. The lightest pellets produce higher muzzle velocities, but quickly run out of steam.

<u>800 fps range:</u> I'd much prefer a gun capable of launching a standard .22 pellet at this speed. It will generate 20 ft·lbs and hit with more noticeable force. Useful range will increase by another five yards as well. Springer choices will narrow, but PCP rifles will remain in the running. A 14.3 grain pellet with an 800 fps MV is pretty useful, and won't be overly loud. It can be zeroed for 30 to 35 yards, and will hammer pigeons or gray squirrels within those distances. If noise is an issue, you'll probably want a sound moderated PCP gun in this power level. I have owned springers that came close to this performance with less noise - most notably the RWS M-48 side lever rifles. You can still buy them, but they won't be small. That power needs a large engine, resulting in a supersized gun with substantial cocking effort.

<u>900 fps and greater:</u> My .22 Air Arms PCP rifle has adjustable power, but usually remains near full output. With a MV of 910 fps from JSB 15.9 grain pellets, it produces 29+ ft·lbs of energy. This increased force is noticeably more decisive, and further flattens trajectory. Some PCP rifles can shoot faster than 900 fps, but I have no need for more airgun punch. In fact, I sometimes crank the power adjustment down for indoor pest control projects. Normally, I stick with the 910 fps setting and zero at 40 yards. A target is in serious jeopardy within that distance, and plenty of crows have turned into lawn darts at much further ranges. Any guns in this power range will greatly benefit from sound moderation. Without this technology, they'll sound more like .22 rimfires!

PRACTICAL RANGE LIMITS

Right now, there are probably readers who are seriously contesting these admittedly arbitrary figures. The Internet is full of stories involving kills at surprising distances, *well* in excess of 50 yards. Many exceed 100 yards, and I don't doubt for a minute that some are actually true. With a rangefinder and accurate PCP rifle, regular hits on prairie dogs should be possible at 100 yards, in calm conditions. This type of shooting involves a target-rich environment with plenty of opportunities for corrected shots. Many hits will result in gophers that disappear down their holes. They'll probably die, but it won't be a humane event. The larger-bore projectiles (.25 caliber or greater) hit much harder, but trajectory may be steeper. Don't forget that for our purposes, ammunition availability will be a major concern. Again, the comments here apply to .22 caliber pellets.

Maximum practical range: The operative word is "practical". It factors in adequate power, accuracy, and trajectory for predictable results. The above velocity ranges should provide some guidance. Here's my take, based on many years of anti-critter airgun operations.

I love my .22 Air Arms M-400. Thanks to its 900 fps velocity, I just aim dead on most targets out to its zero range of 40 yards. At that distance, the rifle will shoot 5/8-inch groups (or better) off a bench rest. I'll hold a touch low (less than an inch) on tiny targets at 27 to 30-yards. At 50 yards, I'll hold around that amount high. The accuracy is still there, but the pellets are running out of steam, so I consider 50 yards my true "practical" limit. Remember: this is with an exceptionally fast 900 fps rifle. Even at this muzzle velocity, beyond 50 yards the pellets begin a rainbow-like descent. There isn't much mass, and the profile develops plenty of drag. Velocity quickly decreases, resulting in severe energy loss. If the exact range is unknown, the odds of a good hit also decrease, while the odds of wounding greatly increase. Don't forget the very real effects of wind, either. Factor in "real world" conditions and your own abilities.

That said, my sidekick Mike and I have made some fairly outrageous hits with our AA-400s. We've toppled crows routinely at 75 yards, using holdover aiming reticles and wind allowance. Some fell out of trees near the 100-yard mark. I had a good education the day I sent my Labrador retriever after a 90-yard victim. He returned with a fairly lively crow that appeared to be well hit. A post-mortem revealed the pellet, which had hit a wing and deflected upward, lodging in its back. The dog thought it was great. The crow didn't, and I wasn't too happy either. Bottom line: that's pushing things beyond their "practical" limit.

If 50 yards is a practical limit for a .22 caliber pellet launched at 900 fps, it stands to reason that lower MVs will shorten this range.

ACCURACY

You really can't make an arbitrary statement about airgun accuracy (or lack thereof). A number of factors can come into play, including gun quality, pellet consistency, shooter technique, and to some extent, powerplant type. You can nail all of these issues but still be defeated by atmospheric conditions. Wind is a major factor, and CO_2 guns are also temperature sensitive. For all types, but particularly the slower guns, bore time is an issue.

Throughout the years, some unofficial standards have evolved for evaluation of accuracy. For centerfire rifles, the range is usually 100 yards. Rimfire rifles are often tested at 50 yards, and airguns at 33 feet. While this distance replicates official target rules, it doesn't reflect field airgun use. We know those practical limits are based largely on power, which can vary from one airgun type to the next. What follows are some broad generalities. Much like vehicle mileage, your results may vary.

Springers: Consistent piston travel *should* result in uniform performance. While pressure and velocity are relatively constant, vibration is a factor. Some die-hard airgunners advocate mastery of spring gun techniques, their contention being that if you can shoot one well, everything else will be gravy. It's a fair argument. Not only is a consistent and light hold required, but also follow-through. Since the gun has a jolt, the ability to let it recoil translates nicely to firearms. Airguns as a whole have less velocity than their powder-burning counterparts, so projectiles spend a little more time inside their barrels. Follow-through not only supports uniform vibrations, but also consistent pellet exits.

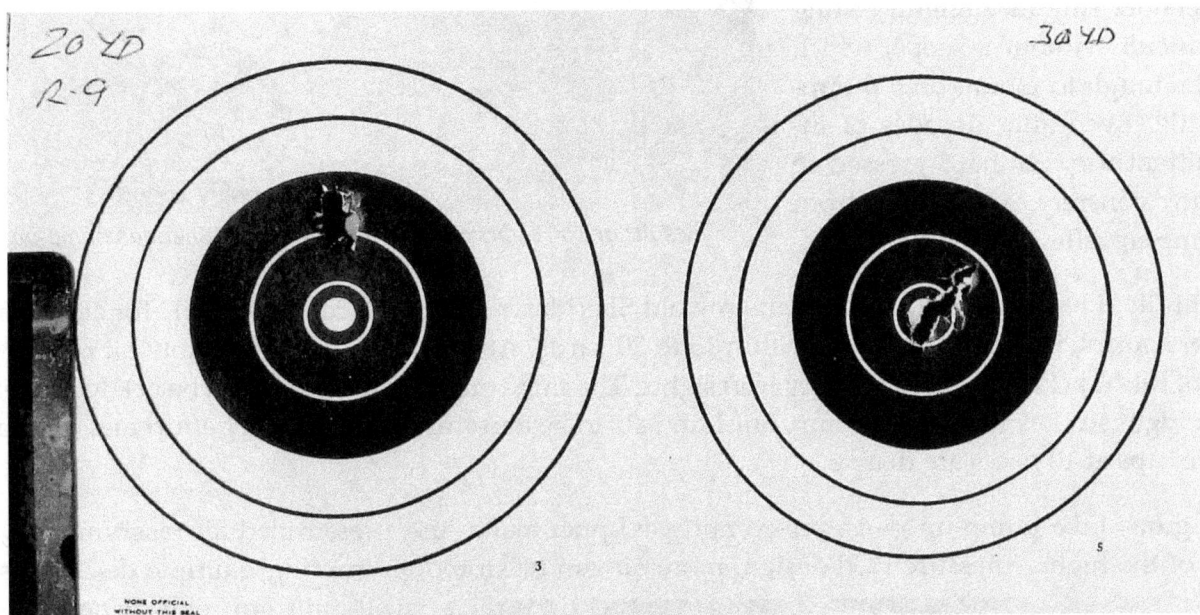

Excellent springer accuracy from a Beeman .22 R-9 at 20 and 30 yards. The groups are five shots each, using Crosman 14.3 grain Premiers.

The ability to accommodate a scope permits precise aiming. However, it will need to be a decent one in order to prevent random zero changes. There is another potential variable inherent to barrel-cocking guns. The scope is mounted to the compression tube (or receiver), but the bore is in a separate, moving part. If both pieces don't align precisely, accuracy will suffer. Some of the extra cost associated with higher quality guns is related to this juncture. The side and underlever designs solve this problem.

Still, with correct techniques and good pellets, a well-built spring rifle can shoot pretty well. In calm air, my .20 Beeman R-1 would put five pellets in dime-sized groups at 35 yards. That's not too shabby! Many other spring guns I've shot grouped into a half-dollar spot at 25 yards. I'd be unhappy with one less accurate, which is a distinct possibility from an inexpensive gun. But even the best of their class won't shoot well with cheap pellets.

It also can take a while for these guns to settle down. You may not realize full accuracy potential for at least 500 shots. During that period you can work on technique. Field positions are worth practicing, but any hard-surface contact (like a fence-post top or tree) is out.

Pump-up pneumatics: Most of these guns are inexpensive, meaning match grade barrels are out. Pumping technique plays a further role, and can cause pressure to vary from shot to shot. Differing velocities will create inconsistent trajectories, which results in greater pellet dispersion. Any meaningful testing is difficult without a scope, which can be tough to mount on a pump-up rifle. Even after decades of intermittent use, I'm hard-pressed to list any concrete expectations from a pump-up rifle.

Results of iron sights and a vintage 5mm/.20 Sheridan pump-up rifle from 15 yards.

Truthfully, I have no idea how accurate my old Sheridan really is. I'll call it "useful" for close-range critter control, including squirrels within 15 to 20 yards. At that distance, it'll reliably hit targets the size of Ritz crackers using the factory iron sights. The same number of pumps will be needed for each shot. Eight strokes are its maximum, but I find six to be a useful compromise of effort and accuracy. Bottle caps at 10 paces are doable.

PCP guns: Like pump-up guns, pre-compressed pneumatics use pressurized air reservoirs. In the case of the higher-pressure PCP design, more air can be stored, permitting multiple discharges. A well-built gun will dispense pressure in well regulated increments, allowing consistent velocities throughout a useful series of shots. The exact amount is dictated by reservoir capacity, pressure, caliber, and valve dynamics.

Near its highest power setting, my .22 Air Arms M-400 provides approximately 45 "useful" shots thanks to its large air reservoir. It can easily shoot extras, but groups will vertically string as pressure subsides. This effect is very noticeable at 40 yards. For maximum accuracy, I'll recharge after around 35 to 37 shots. For pigeon control, I'll run through 45 shots without

Five shots at 65 yards from the Author's .22 Air Arms PCP rifle. The crosshairs were placed on the top edge of the plate to compensate for drop beyond its 40-yard zero.

concern. If the targets are 40-yard paintballs placed on golf tees, I'll refill after 35 shots. Other types may offer only 20 to 30 consistent shots due to smaller reservoirs. In other words, size does matter.

Within its optimum limits, a PCP rifle can be scarily accurate. In fact, mine is possibly *the* most consistent rifle of any type on hand. I have some precise centerfire varminters that will shoot more accurately, but unlike many firearms, the Air Arm's point of impact never varies. It just puts five holes in the same place, day in and day out. As I said, at 40 yards they'll all form in a spot of 5/8" diameter or less. In fact, I'll often see the same size groups beyond 50 yards. Why? I'm not sure, but I do have a few theories.

For starters, barrel heating is nonexistent. Fouling is minimal, too. So is vibration and recoil. Unlike most firearms or spring-powered airguns, I can press my PCP rifle directly against a hard surface. It doesn't seem to affect shot placement during any field-type situations, so suddenly, a fencepost, tree or windowsill becomes a solid shooting aid. A bipod works even better, and won't change zero at all.

Of course, like everything else in life, there's no free lunch. In this case, the costs are dependence on an air source and a significant cash outlay.

TIME TO LOOK AT CATALOGS!

We've looked at the ins and outs of each primary airgun system. It's time to think about the powerplant that most realistically meets our needs. The design aspect may be simple enough. But of course, the devil is in the details…

CHAPTER 5

THE SURVIVAL SPRINGER

If society goes completely to hell, an independent power system will be valuable. A bug-out kit and portable shooting system tie in well, which shortens the airgun list to springers and pump-up pneumatics – that is, unless you have an airgun HPA pump (or at least one pressurized scuba tank) at your new location.

Although plenty of PCP rifles can achieve "magnum" airgun speeds, a spring-powered rifle is both self-contained and capable of a useful degree of power. It will also tend to be quiet, owing to its design. The recent gas piston rifles share similar traits (but may raise concerns about long-term seal integrity). Balancing cost against performance, I'd go with a quality spring rifle. My choice would be a .22 caliber of manageable size and weight. For all but the largest people, these considerations will eliminate the highest powered springers.

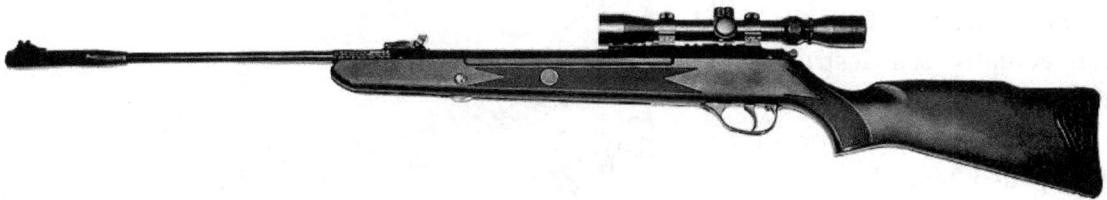

A typical barrel-cocking springer. This one is a .22 Walther Talon Magnum.

BEFORE YOU BUY: SPRING GUN QUIRKS

The spring-powered design is well proven, but it does have a few interesting quirks. We've already taken a cursory look at this design, including its principle advantages and drawbacks. It's now time to more closely examine this useful, but often misunderstood system.

Cocking and uncocking: Long-term spring compression is said to be hard on a gun. Exactly what "long-term" actually means is open to debate, but many knowledgeable shooters will include an overnight period. Heading out with a cocked gun for a day afield constitutes a similar time frame. I avoid periods of more than a few minutes. One alternate technique involves exposing the breech just far enough to load a pellet while leaving the piston uncocked. When ready to fire, a full cocking stroke will ready the gun. It will also automatically place most types on "safe". Some brands can't be returned to "safe" after the button is disengaged. This isn't necessarily as bad as it seems, because if a shot doesn't quickly follow, you may be able to uncock your gun. In most cases, it's not difficult. You swing the barrel (or lever) to its fully cocked position, pull the trigger, and hold on like hell while you ease everything forward. Failure to do so could allow the barrel to snap forward with great force. That would possibly cause an injury, and will probably wreck the gun. Once uncocked, you'll still have a pellet in the breech. The most practical method for removal is to just shoot it out later.

Dry-fire cautions: The muzzle end of most springer or gas piston barrels is choked, meaning the bore has a bit more constriction. This serves to briefly retard a pellet and produce some back pressure in the gun. Don't fire one without a pellet! That air cushion is essential. Without it, the piston head will slam into the front of the compression tube, damaging the gun. Also, during loading, make sure the pellet doesn't fall out of the barrel.

Lubrication warnings: You'll need the right, high flash point, non-petroleum lubricants. Spring or gas piston guns are fairly low-maintenance, but lube on hinges and linkages will greatly prolong their life. The compression tube only needs a couple of drops every 2,000 shots (if that), but it must be a recommended chamber lube. The wrong oil may diesel or detonate, burning up the piston seals. You can buy purpose-built kits containing tubes of spring and compression chamber oils. Whatever you do, don't spray something like WD-40 in the airport!

Special scopes: The piston has considerable mass, developing lots of inertia in the opposite direction of firearms. Most scopes – even higher-end models - are not braced for forward recoil, and can actually self-destruct when mounted on springers. You'll need an airgun-rated optic exactly for this reason. It may also have close-range parallax settings for the shorter shooting distances, inside 25 yards. The same forces that act on the scope can also impart movement to its mounts. The scope and rings may gradually creep rearward with each successive shot and change your zero. The fix is either a scope stop or airgun rings with built in studs. A scope stop is similar to the

These 11mm scope grooves are backed up with holes. They engage anti-creep studs that protrude from the underside of special airgun rings.

lower portion of a ring, and just locks onto the base. Most springers have integral scope bases which accept tip-off type rings. Some of these surfaces have holes designed to mesh with airgun scope ring studs. The trick involves locating everything for adequate spacing and eye relief. While U.S. groove spacing is 3/8-inch, most springers (which are foreign-made) have 11mm bases. In other words, they're a bit wider, meaning not all U.S. rings will fit.

Barrel droop: Here's one more springer bombshell. The barrel-cocking designs often come with decent iron sights that are mounted on the barrel. With younger eyes and good shooting form, they may get you by, but many of us will want to add a scope. This can change things, and not always for the best. If the barrel and cylinder are not on the same axis, you may have problems sighting one in. In that case, shots will probably strike low, even with the scope's elevation cranked all the way up. It just depends on your gun's individual barrel fitting. Luckily, some special "drooper mounts" are sold with built-in corrections.

If you're scratching your head right now, I feel your pain. Your best bet is to buy the gun, scope, and rings from a company specializing in airguns. They've seen it all before and can set you up for little more than what you'd spend at some big box retailer. The other option is to buy a package gun. The only fly in the ointment is quality. Lately, spring-powered air rifles have appeared bearing well-known firearms labels like Remington and Ruger. These guns aren't made by either firm, but are really rebranded imports.

Special shooting techniques: I've already mentioned that springers can be difficult to shoot. Unless held consistently, the jolt from the spring can greatly affect the pellet's point of impact. A springer must be lightly held in a manner promoting uniform recoil, and the correct technique is now referred to as "the artillery hold". The concept has been around for years, but a gentleman we might consider the dean of modern airgunning coined the phrase. Tom Gaylord is that man, and it's an apt description. Much like the stationary carriage on a cannon, during recoil, the actual gun must travel smoothly rearward in a repeatable fashion. As little force as possible should be applied to the airgun. Once mastered, some springers will shoot very well.

The light came on for me more than 20 years ago. I mounted a scope on a potent RWS Model 48 side lever .22, and fired a few offhand shots at a steel plate. From 20 yards, it didn't take long to establish a rough zero, and the ensuing groups looked promising. The next step involved some serious bench

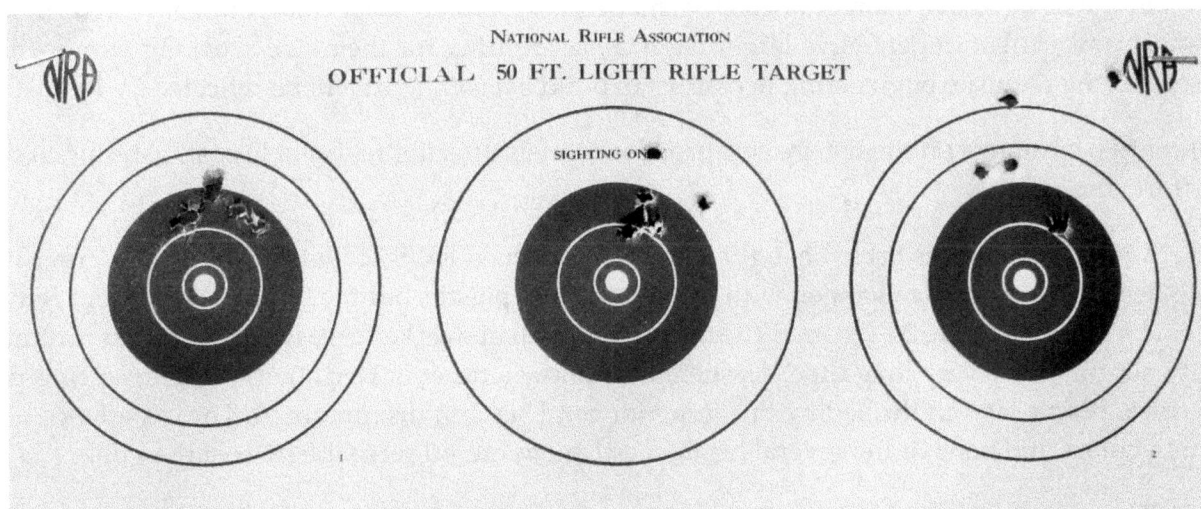

These 30-yard, bench-rested groups were shot using (L-R) artillery hold; a pillow; and sand-bags. Each group consists of 5 Crosman Premier 14.3 grain pellets from a .22 Beeman R-9 spring rifle. Note the elevation shifts related to rest contact.

rest testing, at which point my accuracy immediately evaporated. After checking the gun and scope for rattles or loose screws, I was stymied. On a whim, I launched a few more unsupported shots at the steel plate, and sure enough, they once more landed in a predictable spot. Returning to the bench, I tried shooting off my elbows. Presto, I had a shot group instead of a random pattern. Out came some pillows and towels, and although the final setup was unorthodox, harmony was restored. Without this education it would have been easy to conclude that the rifle was a lemon. Some gun writers still post lousy spring gun accuracy results that were established using conventional protocols.

During sighting in or accuracy assessment, you'll probably need to forget all of the bench rest techniques used for firearms. You can set up sandbags, but you'll need to lightly cradle the gun with your forward hand's fingers, using the front bag only for minimal support. Sometimes a lightly folded cushion of towels on top of the front bag will work instead. You can always try both methods and have some fun at the same time. Each type of gun is an individual. The thing to remember is that any hard gun contact is usually out. This quirk normally eliminates a bipod. Mounting one on a barrel-cocking rifle would be impractical anyway, due to the slot below the forend.

NARROWING DOWN THE CHOICES

If you can live with its quirks, a springer makes sense. Everything is self-contained, so you can grab it and go. The problem is that there are so darned many of them to choose from. The firearm manufacturers have jumped on the bandwagon with rebranded import guns. Others are sold under airgun-specific banners. Regardless, most originate in offshore locales like China, Spain, or Turkey. Prices tend to be reasonable, but quality can vary greatly. For a bit more money one can go with an established airgun maker of German or British origin. The odds of long-term function and ongoing factory service should then increase.

Size and weight are further concerns. An 8 ½ pound gun may not seem overly heavy to a very large adult, but it will carry like a ton of bricks for smaller folks. Add a scope and you'll have an arm load. The most powerful springers have larger engines, accounting for their size. Cocking effort will increase, and the requisite engineering necessary to build a *quality* gun will be reflected by its cost.

The first two springers on the list are compromise models offering reasonable cost, handiness, cocking effort, and velocity.

RWS .22 34-P: A few years back, I bought a synthetic-stocked RWS Model 34 "Panther" to revisit the spring design. Things have changed with the use of more plastic, but the basic RWS concept remains intact. The German-made 34-P comes from the storied Dianawerke firm, which has been producing quality air guns for a very long time. As such, they know a thing or two about building spring-powered rifles. I can't say I'm thrilled by this gun, nor can I say I'm disappointed. The experience was a learning curve, and none of the several headaches I encountered were the fault of the gun.

The 34-P is perfectly serviceable, and has a plastic stock of adult-sized proportions. It has nice lines that will accommodate right or left-handed shooters. The bare rifle weighs 7 ¾ pounds, and its cocking effort is listed as a stout but manageable 33 pounds. An automatic and ambidextrous safety, located on the back of the compression tube, pops rearward to "safe" upon cocking. It can be returned to this position, or the rifle can be uncocked (as previously explained). The two-stage trigger is useable, despite a bit of travel. It's adjustable, but so far, mine has remained untouched.

The fiber-optic, fully adjustable sights are highly visible, and will suffice for many eyes. I was able to zero mine within just a few shots, although at 25 yards, the rear sight needed quite a bit of elevation. I was worried about it bouncing out of zero due to lessened sight spring tension, but it stayed put, providing a nice open sight aiming system.

An 11mm grooved scope base is attached to the receiver. I mail-ordered a very short 6X "Bug-Buster", adjustable objective scope. It had an illuminated mil-dot reticle for holdover aiming. Unfortunately, the included rings were meant for a Weaver or Picatinny base. I had a set of tip-off .22 rings on hand, but the short scope body prevented enough rearward positioning for adequate eye relief. A new BKL one-piece, offset, 3-inch mount solved the problem, nesting firmly against the included RWS stop screw. One concern I had was the screw's ability to resist recoil forces, given its fairly small shank. Before the final mounting, I thoroughly cleaned and degreased all mating surfaces, applying a small amount of blue Loctite to the rails. The two stout cap screws in the BKL mount applied adequate force to keep everything from moving.

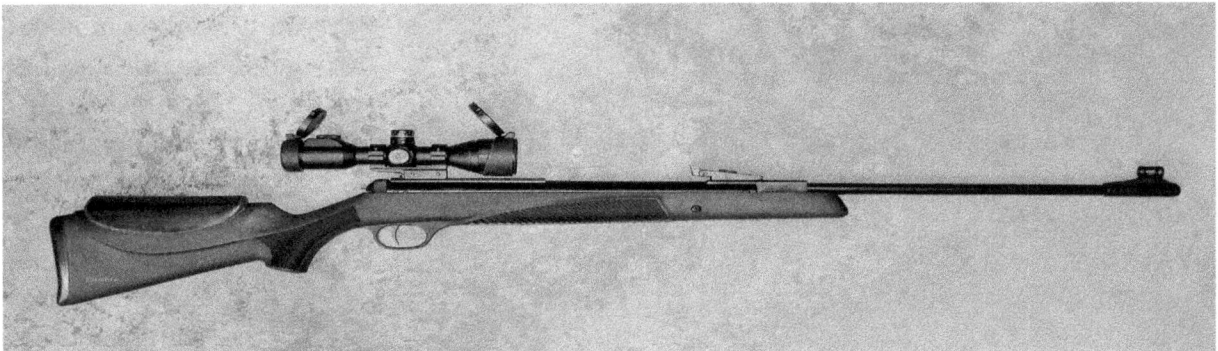

RWS .22 34-P with 6X Bug-Buster scope, BKL mount, and accessory cheek-piece.

Unfortunately, this arrangement positioned the scope higher than I preferred. Fortunately, I had an adhesive cheek piece riser on hand. Guess what? The pad wouldn't adhere securely to the plastic stock. Out came some contact cement. Things were getting *really* complicated.

Luckily, no barrel droop issues were encountered, so the zero process was straightforward. I sighted in for 30 yards. Off the bench, using a very light artillery hold, .22 JSB 14.3 grain lights cut quarter-sized groups. Crosman Premiers in the same weight shot almost as well. Breaking out the chronograph, both pellets clocked 690 fps – not at all surprising and well below the claimed 800 fps muzzle velocity.

A few months later, I switched scopes when an older Burris AO 6X Mini Rimfire/ Airgun Scope became freed up. It easily mounted to the RWS in a spare set of Redfield .22 rings. The rear ring butted up against the small screw head at the rear of the base. Again, for extra insurance, I made sure everything was degreased and tightly secured. The scope was easily sighted in, and also made a great match for the 34-P. The lesson learned? None of the add-ons would have been necessary with more careful shopping.

The wood-stocked RWS-34 appears to have a higher stock, in which case it might be a better match with optical sights. Not only that, but if necessary, a wood stock is easier to shorten. A longer-bodied scope would also provide more latitude for proper eye relief positioning. This combination would also be more likely to work with most rings. The setup shown below is based on these factors. The prices are from the December 2014 Pyramyd Air listings:

Customer-assembled package	
RWS Model 34, barrel-cocking .22 air rifle	$270
Hawke 3-9x40mm AO Sport scope, 1" tube	$ 75
Tech-Force, 1" rings, medium, 3/8" dovetail (set of 2)	$ 12
JSB .22 Diabolo Exact Jumbo Express pellets (tin of 500)	$ 18
	$375

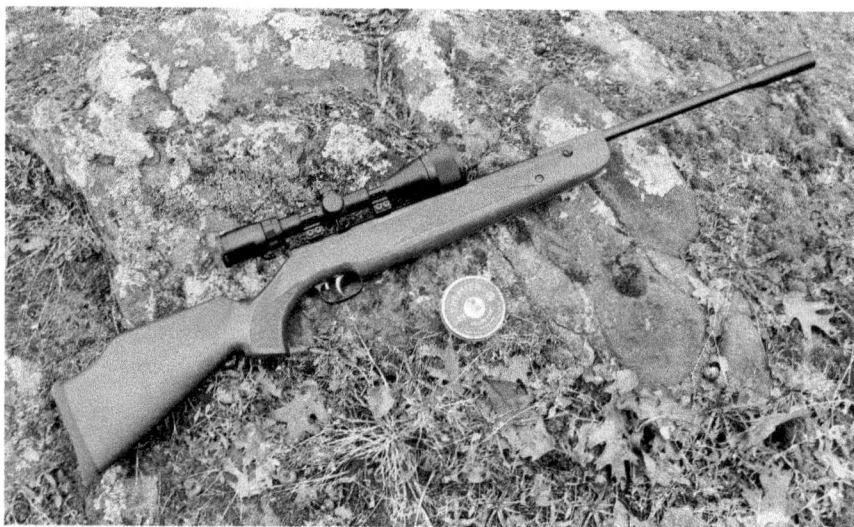

The Beeman R-9. This .22 model is equipped like the Pyramyd Air package, with 1" airgun rings and a Bushnell 4x12 AO scope.

If purchasing the items on this list, you'll need to mount your own scope. The rifle's scope base has small holes on its top surface, designed to accept the anti-creep stud that extends from the bottom of one of the rings. It's good insurance against the whole optical system moving, due to the significant inertial forces developed upon discharge of a springer.

For around the same price, you can buy a pre-scoped package from Pyramyd Air. The mounts will differ, being strong one-piece units, one of which is branded as an RWS. The scope may be durable over the long haul, but prospective buyers would be well-advised to read customer reviews first.

Regardless of the final scope choice, on its lower magnification settings you may see a blurred image of the front sight. I just ignore it. Depending on the scope's exact position, the rear sight might need to be cranked all the way down, or even removed, for necessary clearance. The forward end of the scope didn't contact the rear sight assembly on my P-34, but it partially obstructed the image. I measured the zeroed height of the rear blade using a dial caliper. The correct height was recorded, and the sight was then lowered until it disappeared through the scope. Later, I can always put it back.

Some people look for an airgun with iron sights for use as a backup aiming system. In that case, an airgun like the RWS Model 34 should provide a serviceable air rifle with useful accuracy, a quiet report, and independent but adequate power.

Beeman .22 R-9/HW-95: Herman Weihrauch is another well-respected German airgun maker with plenty of experience. I've owned a bunch of their rifles, and was never disappointed. The adjustable HW "Rekord trigger" is a winner that will likely please as is. The overall build quality is obvious, and the gun is well-suited for optics. A couple different iterations are offered, depending on the importer. Pyramyd Air sells their Beeman version of the HW-built rifle without sights. The barrel has an enlarged "muzzle brake" that really serves as a cocking aid. It does dress up an already great-looking rifle. A set of 1" airgun rings is included, and they have a built-in scope stop feature.

You can buy these guns in .177, .20, or .22 caliber. The .20 is faster, but the .22 hits harder. Velocity is listed at around 740 fps in .22 caliber, but will be in the mid-to-upper 600s, similar to the RWS M-34. Weight is a bit less, at 7.3 pounds. Cocking effort is sometimes listed as 35 or 40 pounds. The 35-pound figure is probably correct, based on my experience. The velocities I've recorded are in line with published data, so the spring in my R-9 must be up to snuff. In any event, it seems much easier to cock than my RWS 34-P.

According to my chronograph, the muzzle velocity of standard weight 14.3 grain .22 Crosman Premiers is about 680 fps. JSB 14.3 grain pellets averaged around 690 fps, and lightweight "Hobby" pellets clocked about 710 fps. I shot some heavier 15.9 grain JSBs through the chronograph, for an average MV of around 630 fps. Although these figures won't match the advertised velocity, they do coincide with published tests.

My R-9 feels smooth during the cocking and firing cycles. Accuracy is good with 14.3 grain .22 pellets, whether JSBs or Premiers. The edge goes to Crosman's 625-count cardboard box type Premiers, which are all struck from the same forming die. These pellets cost around three times as much as the 500-count Crosman Premiers sold in tins. They're also packaged better, with a foam liner in the box to prevent shipping damage. Actually, I use both types, since the mass-marketed Premier Hollow-Points are usefully accurate for plinking or close-range anti-critter operations. Both shoot to the same zero, which is 30 yards.

The R-9's push-button safety will set automatically upon cocking. The rifle's overall build-quality is obvious.

The R-9 handles nicely, and overall, it exudes quality. Instead of an add-on scope base, two deep grooves have been machined directly into its strong receiver tube. A series of holes lie between each groove to accept a scope stop pin. Like most other guns, the safety will be automatically set when the gun is cocked. It's a sideways push-button affair, conveniently located at the rear of the receiver. Once pushed to "fire", it can't just be reset. No problem; you can effortlessly swing the barrel fully down as if you were cocking the gun to reset the button.

Airguns of Arizona sells both R-9 and HW-95 versions. So does Pomona Airguns. A couple of grades and purchase options are offered. The HW rifles shown on the Airguns of Arizona site have good open sights. Either way, you get a nice rifle capable of good accuracy. The R-9/HW-95s really deserve a better scope, so one is shown below:

Customer-assembled package	
Beeman R-9, .22 air rifle (with rings)	$470
Hawke Airmax EV 3-9x40mm AO scope, MAP 6 reticle	$160
JSB .22 Diabolo Exact Jumbo Express pellets (tin of 500)	$ 18
	$648

The scope has a special reticle for ballistic aiming with airgun pellets. If you access the Hawke website, you can correlate it with your gun's trajectory. (You don't absolutely need it, and could save a bit going with their $75 model.) The iron-sighted HW model will appeal to shooters seeking a backup sighting system. I like the uncluttered lines of the brake-equipped R-9. Either way, you'll get a nice gun.

The Beeman version of the R-9 will probably come with rings. An HW-95 may not. These accessories will get you shooting.

Pyramyd Air sells an R-9 package with a pre-mounted Bushnell scope, which may be a "Banner". If so, it'll be clear, and offer some hope of long-term durability:

Pyramyd Air package	
Beeman R-9 Elite Series Combo with scope and rings	$570
Bushnell 4x12 AO Scope in rings (pre-mounted)	Included
JSB .22 Diabolo Exact Jumbo Express pellets (tin of 500)	$ 18
	$588

SUMMARY: THE FIRST CHOICES

RWS sells a serviceable barrel-cocking springer in their Model 34. The synthetic-stocked version is somewhat utilitarian, as reflected by its cost. Those looking for a basic working gun might want to give one some thought. It seems like a reliable choice for quick action against unwelcome pest birds or rodents. The RWS M-34 will also serve well for informal target practice or plinking.

By comparison, the R-9 is more of a deluxe offering. Velocity is similar, but mine was not only more accurate, but clearly more refined. It should satisfy those valuing pride of ownership. The price is commensurate with these attributes, but not exorbitant. The HW-95 is a slightly more Spartan version, but an upgraded HW-95 Luxus is available for R-9 pricing.

First choices: barrel-cocking spring rifles					
Make	**Model**	**Weight**	**MV**	**Cocking effort**	**Price**
RWS	34	7.5 lbs	700 fps	33 lbs	$270
Beeman	R-9	7.3 lbs	700 fps	35 lbs	$460
HW	95	7.5	700 fps	35 lbs	$406
Weights shown are for bare rifles. Pricing is from Pyramyd Air (HW-95 pricing from Airguns of Arizona)					

OTHER SPRING GUN CHOICES

There are other good spring guns worth a look. The list that follows is far from complete but it will point you towards some interesting guns! Be sure to not only look at their velocities, but also their weight and cocking efforts. You'll discover a direct correlation between all three numbers. In most cases, the velocities shown here are real-life numbers based on average weight pellets, rather than advertised speeds. Every gun listed is a .22 for fair comparison.

RWS rifles: Besides the venerable Model 34, other powerful and innovative spring guns are offered. All of these guns are spring-powered. I owned a couple Model 48s, and a similar but now discontinued checkered-stock Model 52. They were a handful, but had plenty of punch and good reliability. I don't have any experience with any of the others, which use three different cocking systems.

The Model 350 is a large and powerful barrel-cocker that requires substantial effort to operate. In fact, it may be too much for some shooters. Those who can manage it will pay more for the privilege. Its increased performance will likely demolish a marginal scope.

RWS Model 350 barrel-cocking air rifle.

The Model 460 is cocked with an underlever, which requires a tad less effort. The separate mechanism also permits use of a rigid barrel, which may contribute to better accuracy. Like the M-350, it's a large rifle. The more innovative M-460 also has a higher price.

RWS Model 460 Magnum under-lever.

The Model 48 employs a stout side lever with a rear-mounted hinge. Drawing it out and rearward in a sweeping arc provides the leverage to cock the piston and expose the breech for loading. A set of ratchet teeth serve as a safety catch to prevent everything from slamming forward if the shooter's grip slips.

RWS Model 48 side-lever rifle, with a rugged one-piece scope base.

The Model 54 is a refinement of the M-48 that uses a unique reciprocating action to help soak up recoil. The barreled action travels in a carriage, which also adds more mass. Nevertheless, its dynamics require a very sturdy scope.

The RWS Model 54 is a refined side-lever rifle with recoilless operation.

None of these "magnum" springers are docile. All have enough recoil to wreck a marginal scope, so you'll need to factor in the extra cost for a decent one.

Other RWS spring-powered rifles					
Model	**Action**	**Weight**	**MV**	**Cocking effort**	**Price**
350	Barrel-cocking	8.2 lbs	800+ fps	45 lbs	$430
460	Underlever	8.3 lbs	800 fps	36 lbs	$550
48	Side lever	8.5 lbs	800 fps	39 lbs	$450
54	Side lever recoilless	9.9 lbs	800 fps	39 lbs	$645

Beeman/HW rifles: The R-9 is just part of a German-built HW family including gas piston and underlever models. Some are also offered in shorter carbine lengths. I have personal experience with a Beeman R-1, RX-2, and HW-97, all of which are *really* nice guns.

The Beeman R-1 is a larger and more robust version of the R-9. The HW-80 is similar to the R-1, with somewhat different styling. The Beeman has sleeker lines, and the HW comes with an excellent set of open sights.

The Beeman R-1/HW-80 is an elegant barrel-cocking springer.

The pretty laminated-stock Beeman RX-2 is even larger, and utilizes a gas piston of sorts. The compression cylinder is sealed, so when the piston is cocked, a highly compressed air "spring" results. It generates plenty of power, but shoots smoothly and can remain cocked. The sudden release generates lots of force, so a rugged scope is advised. The HW-90 is similar but lighter, due to its plainer wood stock. One interesting aspect of these guns is that their air "springs" can be recharged. A small connector can be screwed into the rear of the receiver and hooked up to a PCP-type pump.

The laminated-stock Beeman's RX-2 is a large and powerful barrel-cocking rifle without a spring. The HW-90 version is very similar.

The HW-97, although more sedate, is a really sweet rifle that shoots accurately thanks to its fixed barrel. Cocking is accomplished by an underlever. Wood or laminated stocks are available, including one with eye-grabbing blue shades. The muzzle has an ornamental muzzle brake, and the rifle has no sights. A slightly simpler HW-77 version comes with open sights.

The blue laminated stock of this HW 97-K under-lever rifle is a real attention-getter. Traditionalists will no doubt seek the classic wood-stocked version.

The HW 97-K's cocking arm is firmly secured by a push-button release near the muzzle.

Other Beeman /HW spring and gas piston rifles					
Model	**Action**	**Weight**	**MV**	**Cocking effort**	**Price**
R-1	Barrel-cocking	8.8 lbs	740 fps	36 lbs	$615
HW-80	Barrel-cocking	8.8 lbs	740 fps	36 lbs	$530
RX-2	Barrel-cock/gas piston	9.8 lbs	800 fps	46 lbs	$860
HW-90	Barrel-cock/gas piston	8.8 lbs	800 fps	46 lbs	$640
HW 97-K	Underlever	8.8 lbs	700 fps	35 lbs	$604
HW 77-K	Underlever	8.7 lbs	700 fps	35 lbs	$593
R-series pricing: Pyramyd Air HW pricing: Airguns of Arizona					

Air Arms: These British-built rifles are real eye candy. Not only that, but they can really shoot! Although known for high-performance PCP rifles, Air Arms hasn't ignored the spring gun market.

TX-200: The sport of Field Target involves small steel animal silhouettes shot at unknown distances. Among spring gun shooters, the TX-200 is a highly prized performer. Its fixed barrel is highly accurate, and cocking is accomplished with a separate lever located below the barrel.

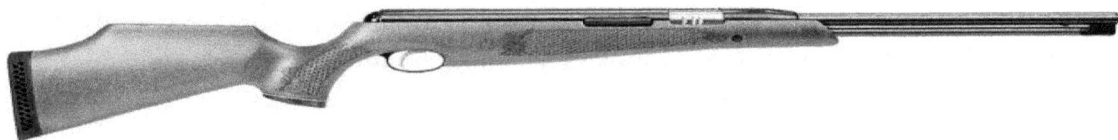

The Air Arms TX-200 under-lever rifle is the darling of springer Field Target competitors.

The Pro-Sport is set up for general field use, and also has an underlever. Its cocking arm has been relocated further rearward so its tip remains hidden inside the forend. The result is a sleek package, but one requiring extra cocking effort. A sling is probably out as well.

The Air Arms Pro-Sport employs an under-lever system, but its cocking arm sit flush inside the forend.

For those who appreciate blued steel and pretty wood stocks, these guns are worth a look. You'll have a hard time buying a better spring-powered gun. They're just not something you'll want to toss inside the nether regions of a truck.

Air Arms spring rifles					
Model	Action	Weight	MV	Cocking effort	Price
TX-200 MKIII	Underlever	9.3 lbs	700 fps	29 lbs	$630
Pro-Sport	Underlever	9.0 lbs	700 fps	40 lbs	$780

Right about now, those with casual interest will be shaking their heads. After all, the flyers, catalogs, and shelves are full of large and imposing airguns for *much* less money. Their claimed velocities greatly exceed the speeds listed so far and, heck, most even come with scopes. We call these mass-marketed products "package guns"…

Big box guns and "package deals": The choices are nearly endless. During a recent big box store visit, I gazed at stacks of airguns in colorful boxes with different labels. Several other shoppers stared at the choices with deer-in-the-headlights expressions. The packaging displayed lavish promises of high octane performance. A large array of pellets was on hand to lend further confusion. It appeared that, with the magic combination, one might launch a .177 projectile to a velocity slightly below the speed of light.

Common brands include Benjamin, Crosman, Stoeger, and Gamo, which are widely sold in retail stores. More guns bear well-known banners such as Browning, Remington, Ruger, or Winchester. At least a dozen other imports are sold in the U.S., the majority being .177 caliber. Many will also include a scope and mounts. I struggled with the idea of listing at least one representative model from this group. Without much firsthand experience, I looked at online reviews. They were mixed, to say the least.

If you buy a package air rifle, you'll get mounts and *some* sort of scope. It might even work…for a while. The scope and mounts may come in separate boxes, requiring consumer installation. I recently shot an inexpensive springer package sold by a well-known firearms manufacturer. Sure enough, it came with an unmounted scope. Its owner had botched the installations and had asked me to make things right. Once everything was properly cinched downs I fired some 30-yard groups, which looked pretty darned good considering what he paid for the gun. It was of Chinese origin and had a lousy trigger, but hey, it worked. I'm just not sure for how long. I'm also not sure what will quit first: the rifle or the scope.

In some cases, the scopes come pre-mounted and may be bore sighted. Eye relief will likely be incorrect, and the scope may even be tilted. In other words, tinkering will probably still be necessary. Some of the "bore sighted" packages might have been adjusted after the factory Christmas or Chinese New Year party. I'd rather spend a bit more for a better scope and start from a clean slate. Knowing that some folks will take the plunge, a few possible candidates are presented, none of which I have any firsthand experience with. One thing they all seem to have in common are mixed customer reviews.

Crosman Optimus? I was feeling a bit guilty over the lack of a package-gun recommendation, so I dropped into a local sporting goods store. They had a large stack of boxed Crosman barrel-cocking rifles on a shelf, and since I knew the owner, I seized an opportunity to get his take on customer satisfaction. He said they had sold roughly 200 without many complaints. All of the feedback was based on .177 models, but the Optimus is also made in .22 caliber. Cocking effort is listed as 30 lbs, and a bare gun supposedly weighs around 6 ½ pounds. The claimed velocity of 950 fps in .22 caliber seems especially optimistic in light of these figures. Either type has a wood stock, fiber-optic open sights, and an unmounted 4X32 Centerpoint scope with 1" rings. The Chinese origin of the Optimus accounts for its very low package price of under $150.

Crosman's Optimus is an example of affordable barrel-cocking springers.

Umarex Octane: A good place to load up on information about this gun is the Pyramyd Air website. You'll read about a potent barrel-cocking rifle powered by gas strut technology. A fairly large collection of customer reviews will provide further information along with some indications of its actual performance. The rifle and its 3-9x40 AO scope are sold as a pre-mounted package, available in both .177 and .22 calibers. Following our general theme, the larger bore will be referenced here. The Octane is advertised as capable of achieving 1250 fps with light alloy pellets, but most folks will shoot heavier lead types up to 18 grains. Muzzle velocity will then run closer to 800 fps, although the standard weight 14.3 grain types may clock 850 fps or more. This kind of velocity comes at a price, which includes size, weight, and cocking force. The required effort is listed as 42 pounds, and the overall weight shown is a hefty 9 ½ pounds. It's clearly not a gun for any smaller-framed shooters. The synthetic stock is proportioned accordingly and configured as a thumbhole type. An interesting feature is Umarex's muzzle-mounted silencer. The safety is located within the Octane's trigger guard, requiring a rearward motion to place it in the "fire" position. Its proximity to the trigger blade may be of concern to some users, who often report a mediocre trigger pull. Considering the package price of $220, perfection is likely elusive, although the three-year warranty is somewhat reassuring.

The Umarex Octane gas-spring rifle includes a pre-mounted scope.

A novelty gun – the Gamo Viper Express Air Shotgun & Rifle: This barrel-cocking springer is an airgun alternative to a .22 rifle loaded with rat-shot. The Gamo Viper shoots tiny doses of #9 shot from small, flanged, plastic "cartridges" at a claimed velocity of 750 fps. The barrel is a .22 caliber smoothbore, but it can also shoot standard .22 pellets through a different brass insert. The breech is scalloped with finger recesses to permit removal of either cartridge, and the gun won't work without them. The unrifled barrel will not produce stellar accuracy with pellets, but it should be adequate to tip over cans within 15 yards. That's also the absolute maximum range for its tiny 17 grain shot charge. A more realistic distance would be 10 yards or less. Instead of sights, much like a true shotgun, the Viper has a ventilated rib barrel with a bead front sight designed for pointing. The shot cartridges are capped on both ends with plastic wads that exit with the birdshot. At around $8 for a box of 25 shells, they're as expensive as standard 12 gauge loads! However, inventive users could reload those using homemade wads and lead shot. Balled up tufts of cotton will supposedly work in place of wads. The Viper is mainly a curio. It lacks adequate performance for use on game, but might be useful against small pests at very close range. It may also have some training value for new shooters. We'll examine a way to use the Viper in the upcoming training chapter. Cost for the gun is around $200.

The Gamo Viper .22 airgun can shoot .22 pellets or special shot-shells through its smooth-bore barrel.

Gamo Viper's shot-shells and the special adapter needed to shoot .22 pellets.

Used spring guns: I recently visited a large and well-known firearm retailer. A rack full of air rifles was on the floor, accessible for handling. I had my eye on a used Beeman R-9, which I quickly discovered was cocked. So were most of the other spring guns, most of which had trigger locks. I'm sure, if possible, they would've been dry-fired. Some probably had been, and I doubt the sales clerk knew the difference. God only knows how long they were cocked. Prices were lower than new guns, but not by much. In this instance, I would have saved $35 to gain an airgun with problems. Unless you know the previous owner, you're safer buying a new gun.

Left-handed shooters: Many spring gun designs are inherently ambidextrous. The barrel-cockers often fit this bill, but left-handed shooters can still run into problems. Some of the most attractive stocks have pronounced cheek pieces, and most are designed for righties. Left-handed models are sometimes offered, but usually for a bit more cost. It pays to check before ordering!

Specification notes: If you jump back and forth between airgun websites, you'll discover disparities in weight, velocity, and pricing. Most of the European and UK wood-stocked guns are built from beech, and walnut is sometimes listed as a higher-priced option. Variations in wood density no doubt account for some of the weight discrepancies. Synthetic stocks will vary as well. Once again, advertised velocities are often "optimistic". Instead, I decided to show figures from actual users (including me). Prices can really bounce around due to currency exchange rates and manufacturer/dealer relationships. I stuck with a few familiar sources, but there are plenty of other dealers.

CHAPTER 6

HOW ABOUT A PUMP-UP AIRGUN?

I have a 1960s vintage 5mm pneumatic Sheridan Blue Streak leaning in the corner, and it's still going strong! Maintenance consists of a few drops of lube on the hinges and seal every year. It's not a high-performance gun, so 30 weight motor oil works. During standby periods, a couple of pump strokes help seal the valves against dust to maintain their integrity.

Once in a while, I use it to blow an unwelcome wasp to smithereens in the house. Eight pumps will do the job, minus a pellet. That's also the maximum recommended shooting charge. Add more air and you run the risk of creating a condition called "air lock". When that happens, the internal hammer can't overcome air pressure against the valve. In other words, it's wise to heed the manufacturer's recommended limits!

VARIABLE POWER

I've used as few as three pumps to dissuade unwelcome four-legged visitors (don't use less or you may lodge a pellet in the barrel). A more recent incident involved a gray squirrel determined to empty the bird feeder on our deck. I set up shop at a window, twelve yards away. Before long, I watched a low-velocity 5mm flat point pellet arch into his butt. The squirrel vacated the feeder with urgency, but suffered no permanent disabilities. I know this because, being a squirrel, he was persistent. Sure enough, he was back the next day for round two. The same thing happened on the third day, only this time, his approach resembled someone on mine detector duty. Eventually, he lapsed into sunflower rapture for his daily 3-pump hint. Luckily, he got the message. Day Four was scheduled as an eight-pump event. No doubt there are thousands of such stories, because pump-up guns have been around for decades. Indeed, one great advantage of the design is its variable power.

A decades-old Sheridan pump-up pneumatic, appropriately configured for can perforation.

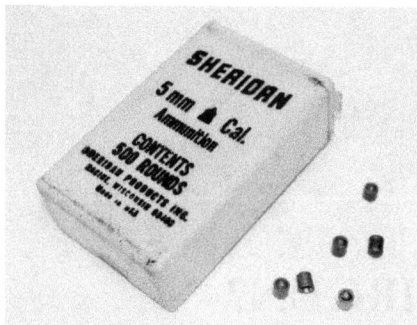
The 5mm Sheridan shot a somewhat unusual .20 caliber cylindrical pellet.

Most pump-up guns are single-shot bolt-actions with a forend/pumping arm that is hinged near the muzzle. With each stroke a linkage drives a piston located in a compression reservoir underneath the barrel. The normal maximum of 8 to 10 pumps will drive a .22 caliber pellet to around 625-650 fps, a velocity adequate to dispatch squirrels inside 20 yards. For tipping over cans, 4 -5 strokes will suffice. A few will also fire BBs from a gravity-fed magazine, along with singly-loaded .177 pellets.

SCOPE LIMITATIONS

Since each shot requires a separate pumping process, extended shooting sessions require much physical effort. To obtain the necessary leverage, the shooter's strong hand will encircle the receiver. The support hand cycles the forend and both hands are drawn closely together to complete a stroke. At first it's an awkward procedure but, with practice things smooth out.

Unfortunately, the grip required to pump the gun eliminates receiver-mounted optics. I still have a Sheridan scope base that clamps around the barrel. I once mounted a small rimfire scope, which interfered with pumping. Grasping it seemed like a great way to throw everything out of whack, and that's exactly where my hand wanted to go. I just didn't care for the whole Rube Goldberg arrangement. A longer eye relief, low-powered pistol scope seemed plausible, the idea being to slide the mount forward of the receiver. Some shooters use a similar centerfire "scout scope" system for quick close-range work. The concept has never caught on in a big way, and is something either loved or hated. Pyramyd Air offers such a package for those seeking better aiming precision. We'll come back to it, momentarily.

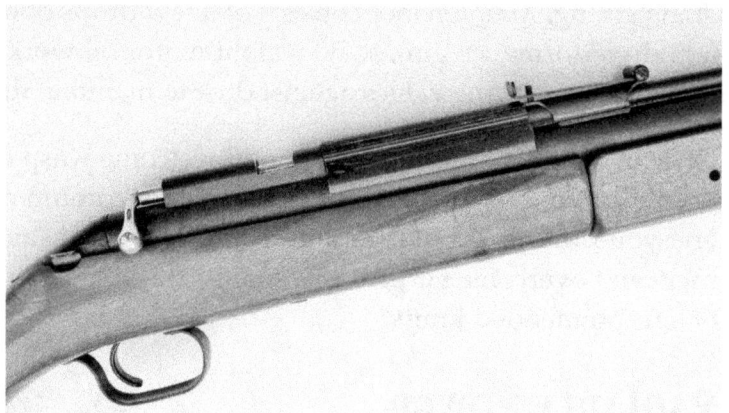
The protective plastic guard between the bolt and rear sight is for grasping.

The hand positioning needed to comfortably charge a pump-up rifle is problematic with scopes.

Pump-up pneumatic air rifles are also fairly loud. They're not as bad as a .22LR, but they are louder than a .22 Short. Any residential neighbors will probably know when one is going off. On a more positive note, you can leave them pumped up. Also, for all practical purposes, pneumatic guns are recoilless, so those contemplating optics won't need to worry about airgun-specific types.

THE PUMP-UP PICK

During the post-WWII period, guns of this type were sold by Sheridan, Benjamin, and Crosman. The market was directed primarily towards younger shooters, but they were nicely made, with real wooden stocks and blued metal. My old Sheridan has survived several decades, and the brand name continues as well. You can still buy a .20 caliber Sheridan rifle, now sold through Crosman. It's a bit different from my old "Blue Streak" model, although not by all that much. The tang-mounted rocker safety has been replaced by a push-button on the trigger guard. Instead of a steel stamping, that part is now a plastic assembly. Fortunately, the wood stock and pumping arm remain.

Benjamin's Model 392: Crosman absorbed this all-American brand and streamlined the multi-stroke airgun line. A Benjamin pump-up facsimile of the newest Sheridan is still available in .177 and .22 caliber. The latter choice will serve our purposes, and has the same basic mechanism. It's usually sold as just a rifle, without any accessories.

Benjamin's Model 392 .22 multi-stroke pneumatic.

Customer-assembled system	
Benjamin Model 392, multi-stroke pneumatic .22 air rifle	$170
Crosman .22 Premier Hollowpoint 14.3 grain pellets (tin of 500)	$ 10
	$180

M-392 scope package: Pyramyd Air must have been thinking about the scout scope concept when they put together an in-house package. A video details this combination on their website. The scope and base are also available separately, for a bit more money.

Pyramyd Air rifle and scope package, with separate tin of pellets	
Benjamin Model 392, multi-stroke pneumatic .22 air rifle package	$260
(includes BSA 2X pistol scope and Intermount)	
Crosman .22 Premier Hollowpoint 14.3 grain pellets (tin of 500)	$ 10
	$270

The latest Intermount consists of two split base assemblies that clamp around the barrel. Each top surface is machined for 3/8" tip-off rings that fit grooved rimfire receivers. Before final tightening, each base can be slid along the barrel for spacing to match various scope bodies. The bad news is the extra scope height imposed by the bases and rings. This would drive me nuts (okay, even more nuts) for two reasons. First, a proper stock cheek weld wouldn't be possible, and second, the barrel/scope offset would require hold off allowances. Those less picky might live with this arrangement, gaining a durable optically-sighted rifle for not much money. An add-on cheek piece might fix the scope height issue.

Here are the components needed to mount a BSA 2X pistol scope in a forward, barrel-mounted location. Pyramid Air carries them.

A Benjamin Model 392 scoped in a more conventional manner, which poses pumping challenges.

A third Benjamin M-392 aiming option is a Williams M-64 Receiver Sight. It will provide more aiming precision than the factory open sights, without any attendant scoping issues. The cost is $40, and those with decent vision may want to give one a try. This sight supposedly works with the front blade, so increasing its height shouldn't be a problem. Just buy it and screw it on.

The Custom Model 392 ACP MK II: Airgun of Arizona lists a very unusual, modified Benjamin pump-up pneumatic rifle. It's not a repeater in the true sense of the term. "ACP" stands for "air-conserving pumper". In a sense, this modified M-392 is a hybrid PCP rifle. More than one shot is possible from one series of pump strokes, due to valve and striker modifications. The pneumatic system then be-

The Air Venturi Williams M-64 Peep Sight is a simple aiming improvement.

comes much more efficient, and also quieter. Depending on how the gun is used, subsequent shots require only minimal pumping to restore its power. A visual indicator is provided to prevent over-pressurization, which could lead to an air locked rifle. All in all, it's a clever design, priced accordingly higher at $340.

OTHER PUMP-UP GUNS?

The parent company, Crosman, is a well-known airgun maker that offers more affordable pump-up rifles. They're also made with lots of plastic parts. Since many land in the hands of junior shooters, they must compete with other low-cost brands. A few are loose cosmetic renditions of an AR-15 rifle. Besides their immortal line of spring-powered BB guns, Daisy still sells an inexpensive assortment of pump-up "PowerLine" .177/BB guns. "Black Ops" just unveiled a similar gun. None are really serious contenders for our purposes.

Webley, a possible second choice: A few foreign and intriguing multi-stroke rifles have come and gone. The newest arrival is Webley's Rebel, and a .22 caliber version of this British rifle is available. Muzzle velocity is

Another possible contender is Webley's .22 Rebel pump-up rifle.

similar to the Benjamin M-392, at somewhere south of 700 fps. The overall design is familiar as well, although a synthetic stock is used. For those who can figure out how to scope and pump one, the Rebel has a grooved receiver. Cost is listed at less than $120 by Airguns of Arizona.

MULTI-STROKE TIPS

A pump-up design won't be the first choice for those seeking top accuracy. The scope mounting headaches and pressure variables are hindrances, but accuracy can often be improved with consistent pumping.

Consistency: Make sure the forend is fully extended between each stroke. At that point, you'll hear a small hiss as air is drawn through an inlet port. A brisk but steady return will build consistent air pressure within the gun's air reservoir. With only a bit of practice, you should be able to develop a rhythm. This consistent pumping technique will result in uniform pressure and velocity, for less vertical shot dispersion.

If accuracy falls off, try cleaning the barrel. It may have accumulated a thin layer of fouling, which can easily be removed. A patch or two, lightly coated with Break-Free, should wipe out this layer. A couple extra dry patches can follow. The breech may be too small for use of a pull-through system, so a rod will likely be necessary. Since cleaning will need to occur through the muzzle, extra caution should be exercised to prevent damage. Fortunately, you won't need to do this often.

Note: Be sure to do this chore with an unloaded and depressurized gun!

Projectiles: The breech area is fairly small, so it's easy to accidentally flip a pellet during loading. If it winds up backwards in the barrel, you can just shoot it out. The same remedy will probably work if you somehow load two pellets. Pump the gun to its maximum so they don't lodge partway down the barrel. Too few pumps can also stick a pellet, and the remedy is the same. An attempt to reuse a shot pellet can lead to bigger problems. Odds are it will become seriously stuck. Other foreign projectiles are a recipe for disaster, and could damage the fragile rifling. Stick with the recommended projectiles, and trouble-free shooting will continue.

Pressure: A pump-up gun will work best at a range of somewhere between 4 and 8 strokes. Keep pumping and you may "air lock" its release valve, tying up the gun. The bolt cocks a spring-loaded striker that knocks it open. Sometimes, repeat cocking and trigger pulls can gradually reduce pressure. If it finally fires, give it another shot. Some residual pressure may remain, and this step should empty the reservoir. Without pressure, the only sound will be the striker hitting the valve. Anytime you pull the trigger, make sure the bolt is fully closed. That will help prevent its cocking lug from being damaged by impact with the striker.

Storage: As mentioned previously, it's a good idea to store a pump-up gun with a couple of strokes' worth of air. The valves will then seat to keep out dust. Before any actual shooting begins, you can point your gun in a safe direction and dry-fire it. It won't hurt a multi-stroke design a bit, and the snap will indicate it's been holding air. Afterwards, just pump it up normally and begin shooting. Eventually, the seals will dry out and begin leaking without lubrication. Crosman "Pellgunoil" provides cheap maintenance, and it doesn't take much to maintain a pneumatic. Penetrating or detergent oils and gun solvents can attack the valves. Read the owner's manual, and life will be good.

Safety: I like to pump the gun first, and load it last. It just seems safer. In fact, placing the gun on "safe" is always a good idea. Even without a pellet, the gun can cause some damage. The blast of air has considerable force that could cause a serious injury at close range. Earlier, I mentioned blasting wasps. Just think what the same pressure could do to an eyeball!

I also described an anti-squirrel operation, conducted at three pumps. The pellet will be visible in flight, and look relatively harmless. Well, it's not! Anything on the receiving end will get a serious jolt. A gray squirrel has really tough hide. You can skin a rabbit without a knife. Try that with a gray and your fingernails will come off first. The one I educated was probably better off at three pumps than eight, but there's no guarantee. Thinner skinned animals could easily sustain a mortal injury, and birds will almost certainly die.

Domestic animals and humans are strictly off-limits. Treat a low-velocity pellet as a bullet. Handle the gun with the same care required of a firearm. Then have fun!

CHAPTER 7

PRE-CHARGED PNEUMATICS

APCP gun is not unlike a multi-stroke pneumatic. Typically, it will have some sort of small bolt-action receiver with a barrel attached, and this assembly will be mounted above a large tubular air reservoir. Drawing the bolt rearward will cock a spring-loaded striker. Squeezing the trigger will release the striker to impact a valve, metering high-pressure air into the barrel. The big difference between a pump-up design and PCP gun is the available amount of pressure. Multiple shots at relatively high velocity require a large amount of pressurized air, way more than could be comfortably managed by a series of forend strokes.

The challenge involves stuffing in enough air from some external source, which complicates matters. A workable system requires extra equipment that elevates cost. Since high-pressure air is serious business, the actual gun must be well-engineered. Its cost alone may equal or exceed that of an excellent, ready-to-shoot spring rifle. Considering expense and the need for an external air source, a PCP design is probably not the best choice for any incidental users, or those in full bug-out mode.

TAKING THE PCP PLUNGE

Some gun people are fascinated by technology and peak performance. In the world of airguns that's where pre-charged rifles shine. One obstacle to overcome is cost. For many prospective buyers, there's also the confusion factor. Exactly what in the heck is needed to get one up and running? I was in that boat. After much Internet research, I finally got a handle on the PCP basics. A call to Steve at Pomona Airguns filled in the few remaining blanks. Many of the comments that follow will apply to pre-charged guns in general.

Air Arms PCP rifles: The rifle I chose was a British-made Air Arms Model 400. In the decade that has since passed since its purchase the pre-charged market has blossomed, resulting in more choices at lower prices. However, I have no regrets. Quality, accuracy, velocity, and ample air capacity were my four main considerations, all of which were satisfied. The rifle-length airgun that showed up on my doorstep was a grabber, right out of the box. The metal-work was first rate with great bluing. The stock had nice lines with a decidedly European flare, including a Schnable tip, and high cheek piece designed for optics. I chose a beech stock, but it was far from plain, bearing plenty of ornate but useful checkering. The pride of ownership aspect was definitely present. Despite the spate of recent competitors, when the itch for a second carbine-length PCP gun struck, I stuck with the Air Arms brand.

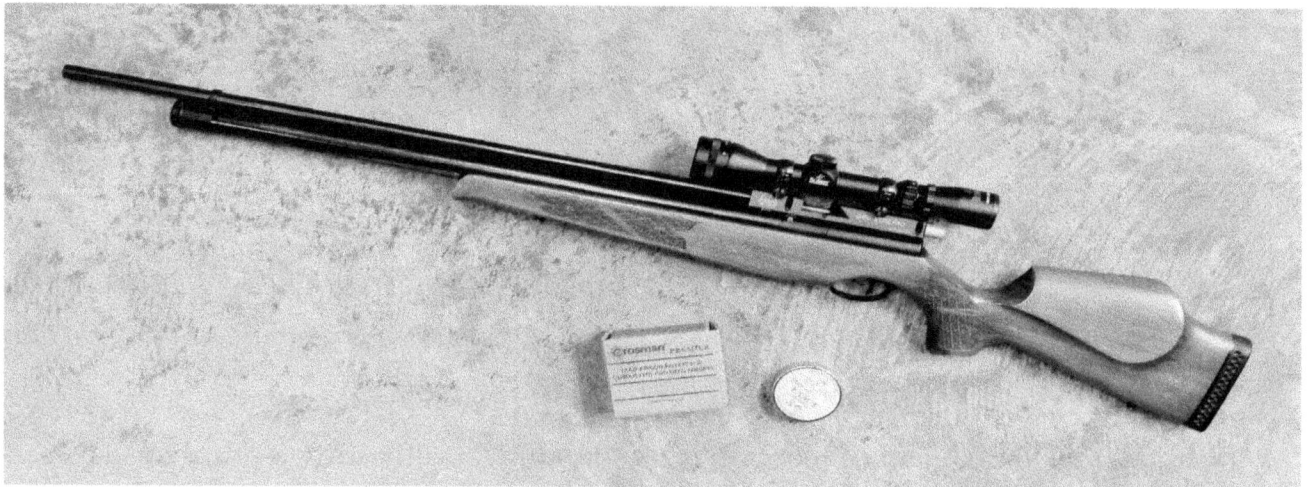

Air Arms Model 400 ERB .22 single-shot pre-charged rifle. It has now morphed into a Model 500.

My initial M-400 ERB .22 was the longest of three configurations. Carbine-length and mid-sized versions were also available but, since hunting was in the cards, I sought adequate air-capacity to support an excursion afield. As it turns out, I have that in spades; getting up to 45 useful shots between each fill. Actually, I could get even more by turning down the pressure with its graduated rheostat. Instead, I choose to run the gun near peak power, recording 910 fps with 15.9 grain JSB pellets.

The M-400 is a single-shot version, but Air Arms also sells repeating models that feed from neat little rotary magazines. This indirectly ties in with the safety, which is just a small push-button located on the trigger blade. Air Arms rifles are known for their great triggers, so fiddling with a safety in that location makes me nervous. In fact, I seldom use it. Instead, if a shot is delayed, I simply open the bolt and firmly draw it beyond its cocking point. I then squeeze the trigger, while carefully controlling the bolt as it eases forward under striker spring tension. At that point the gun

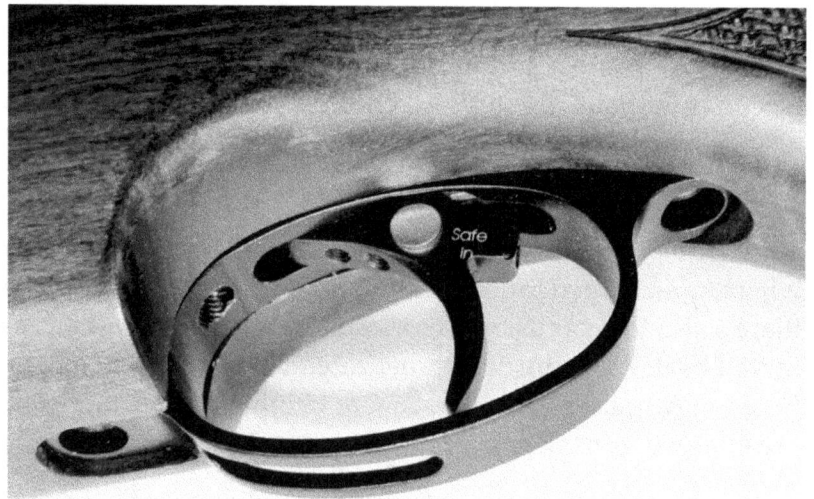

Air Arms safety button shown in the "fire" position.

is uncocked with a pellet in its barrel. Another quick tug on the bolt will re-cock the striker whenever desired. However, this won't work with most repeaters (including the Air Arms PCP rifles), because subsequent cocking will feed another pellet and cause a double-load. The fix is simple: just carefully engage the safety.

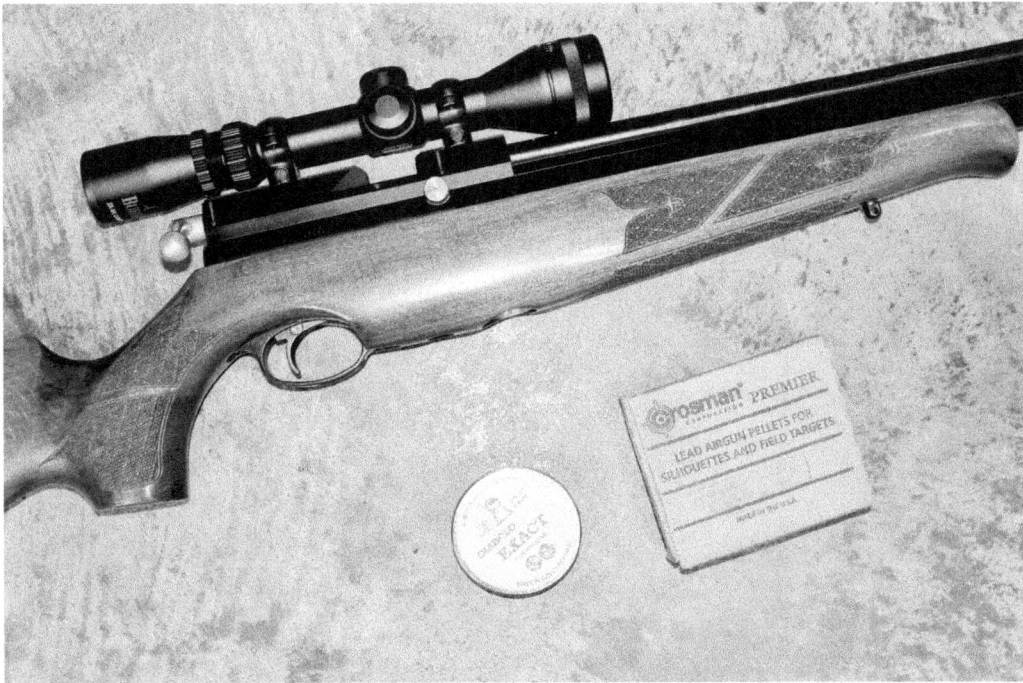

Air ArmsM-400 single-shot action showing the bolt and power-adjustment knob.

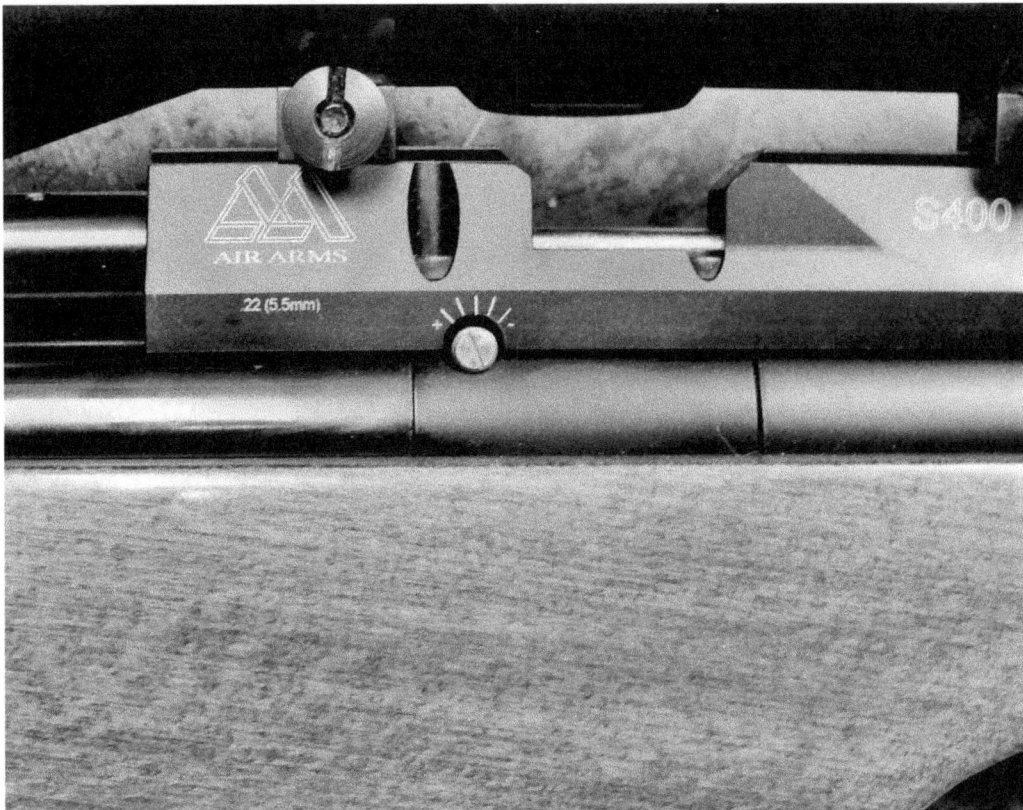

Left side of the M-400 breech, showing the power adjustment reference scale.

My newest carbine-length PCP is a 10-shot Air Arms Model 410-S, again from Pomona Airguns. It has a shorter barrel and air reservoir, but uses the same stock. The traditional airgun-type bolt has been replaced by a small side arm for extra leverage. Some people complained that the bolt-action variant was difficult to cock, and although it never bothered me, the latest iteration is almost effortless. Swinging the side arm out and rearward not only cocks the valve striker, but also cycles the rotary magazine to align pellets with the barrel. Like a Smith & Wesson revolver, it rotates counter-clockwise (or anti-clockwise if you're British). As the lever is returned, the bolt passes through the magazine, shoving a pellet into the breech. As long as the bolt is forward, the magazine is held captive.

The Air Arms M-410 SL Carbine FAC with a 10-shot rotary magazine.

AA M-410 cocking arm, which also cycles its rotary magazine.

Removal of the magazine is as easy as swinging the cocking lever rearward and just plucking it out. I have a spare, which permits quick reloads. Sling swivel studs were added to both Air Arms rifles. After a magazine change, when time permits, I can sling the repeater and reload the empty one. The "cylinder" (think revolvers) is a fairly flat disk with ten chambers. It rotates within a thin housing that has a loading port. As each empty chamber is aligned with the port, a pellet can be dropped in. Instead of loading all ten chambers, I leave the last one empty. That way, a pellet can't inadvertently pass through the housing and fall out. After insertion into the rifle, closing the bolt will cause it to pass through the empty chamber, trapping the magazine in place. With the safety on, the rifle is doubly safe to carry afield. Simply re-cocking the rifle will seat a pellet. If, after firing a shot, another isn't imminent, I'll just leave the gun uncocked and skip the safety. Anytime it's cocked, the safety is engaged, and with company, it is always on.

If the whole process sounds a bit fiddly, well, it is. By comparison, my M-400 single-shot is a no-brainer. The only hassle with either involves handling the pellets. As a right-handed shooter, I normally load the single-shot rifle with my left hand. Even in .22 caliber, the pellets are small enough to require some dexterity. Like many other things, though, there is a certain knack to it.

Air Arms 10-shot .22 magazines: the bolt passes through the loading port to trap a magazine securely in place. The right-hand magazine is a nice aftermarket unit sold by RC Machine.

AA M-410 breech and power scale. Surprise: the graduations are reversed from the AA M-400 single-shot version.

As for the repeating M-410, I spent $20 on a single-shot loading tray. It replaces the magazine and inserts similarly. Using this device, pellets are rolled into a trough-like recess from the left side, where they align with the breech and bolt tip. I quickly found out that this is easier said than done. It takes care to avoid tipped or backwards pellets, and good light helps. However, without either this gizmo or a magazine, loading would be much more difficult. I rate it as an accessory worth owning, and leave it in the rifle during storage.

Air Arms has since consolidated and upgraded their M-400 line to a new M-500 series. They're very similar, and all incorporate the side arm cocking feature. Like the previous models, the M-500 rifles are single-shots, and the M-510s are repeaters. Either can be had as full-size rifles, or carbine-length repeaters. There is even a model with dual air reservoirs, arranged like a side-by-side shotgun.

An RC Machine single-shot adapter, with a pellet ready to seat.

Here's the coolest part: like many of the current PCP genre, the Air Arms rifles have a barrel shroud (or moderator), which cuts the muzzle report to just a mild snap, only slightly above the sound of a heavy-duty stapler. The barrel appears to be quite thick, but its outside appearance is deceiving. The actual barrel is much thinner and located within a metal sleeve. This "shroud" extends beyond the muzzle and, back by the receiver end, there is a small port that vents off residual air pressure. It makes a big difference in the report, too. Those plain-barreled pneumatic rifles I've shot sounded really nasty by comparison.

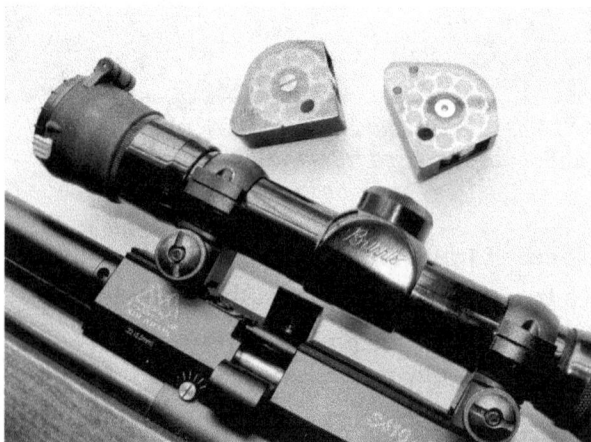

Closing the bolt will shove the pellet home and secure the adapter. It can be plucked out and exchanged for a magazine by simply withdrawing the bolt.

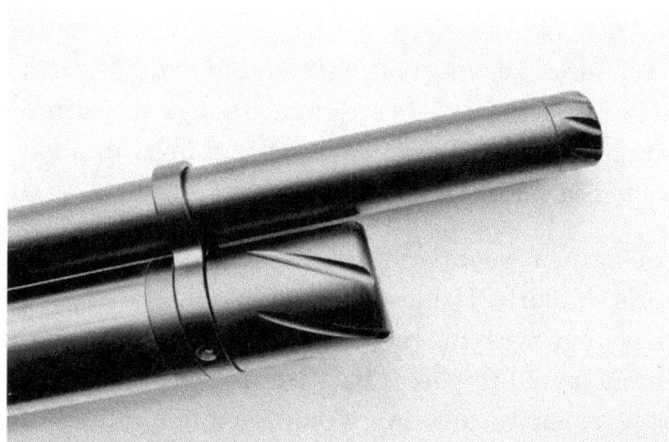

The "barrel" is actually a noise-reducing shroud, fitted with threaded cap. The larger cap protects the fill port located on the end of the pressure tube.

With PCP designs, recoil is nonexistent, so special scopes are not required. The hold sensitivity of a springer is gone as well. In fact, accuracy is phenomenal. My AA M-400 rifle-length airgun prints

5-shot groups as small as ½" at 40 yards. Sighted in at that distance, I just aim dead on at most targets in between. The AA 410 Carbine is handier due to its shorter length, but the tradeoff is a shorter air reservoir that somewhat limits useful shots. I can overcome this slight handicap thanks to the power rheostat, combined with lighter pellets. Instead of 910 fps, I run it at 820. Lighter 14.3 grain pellets are used instead of 15.9 grain JSB Heavies. These steps help flatten out trajectory while maintaining my 20 ft·lb small game preference. Instead of zeroing at 40 yards, the carbine is sighted in for 35 yards. The small concessions result in a still highly effective package that permits plenty of shots between top-offs. I'm good for at least 35 shots during pest bird shoots. The latest twin-cylinder Air Arms offerings provide lots of extra air for extended shooting sessions.

It's all right to leave these guns charged, too. Most amazingly, I can fill them and leave them for weeks on end. They don't leak a bit. A manometer (pressure gauge) in the bottom of the forend indicates the air charge. The small, recessed dial is graduated in increments up to 250 bar. You'll see this term used often with pre-charged pneumatics. The maximum fill pressure of the Air Arms rifles is 200 bar, or 2900 psi. When the needle falls to just above 100 bar, it's time for a recharge. Unscrewing a large cap on the end of the air reservoir reveals the filling apparatus. A proprietary yoke is slipped over its end, connecting the gun to an air source. A short shot of high-pressure air then quickly recharges the gun.

Although the M-400 ERB is large, it isn't excessively heavy. The size results from an extra-long air cylinder. The generous 321 cc capacity accounts for the large number of useful shots. I can get roughly 7 fills, or 300 shots, from a scuba tank

This on-board pressure gauge or "manometer" is graduated in units of pressure known as BAR. Although a great indicator of remaining air, don't use it to charge a gun.

PCP fill system consisting of a scuba tank, yoke, hose, and fill adapter.

charged to 3200 psi. This assumes the gun is always shot through its full useful charge. But more often, I might use just a portion in a shooting session. In that case, the subsequent fill requires less air, so a scuba tank actually seems to last quite a while.

If all of this seems too good to be true, well, it's not – except for two things: cost and extra equipment. Not only is an Air Arms gun expensive, but a scuba tank, hose, and yoke assembly is required. I could have gone with an airgun-specific pump instead, but the total price would have been similar.

Equipment prices haven't decreased; the good news is that PCP costs have come down quite a bit during recent years. I paid nearly $900 for my AA 400, but some decent guns are now available for less than half of that. Let's look at equipment first.

REQUIRED GEAR

Obviously, you'll need a PCP gun. It will probably come with a fill adapter designed for the gun's air inlet. We'll start at the gun end, with this small and inexpensive part:

Fill adapter: This is the connection between the gun and a high-pressure air hose. Make sure the PCP gun you order has one! The designs vary depending on the gun. Some are probes that deliver air by simply plugging them into the gun's air reservoir. Once inserted, the gun can be pressurized from a scuba tank or pump. Others adapters attach to a nozzle at the end of the gun. That part might even be a standard Foster male QD air hose fitting, which will usually be protected by a removable cap.

The Air Arms adapter is a brass collar that slips over a corresponding tubular extension on the gun's air reservoir. Each piece has a port and, when both are properly aligned, air will flow into the gun. The adapter collar has a male Foster connector. Like many standard air tools, it can pop on or off the hose by simply retracting a spring-loaded female collar. That's a nice feature for those contemplating a second gun with a different adapter system. You can just snap on the adapter of your choice, or switch it to the coupling on a pump system. Adapters are relatively inexpensive.

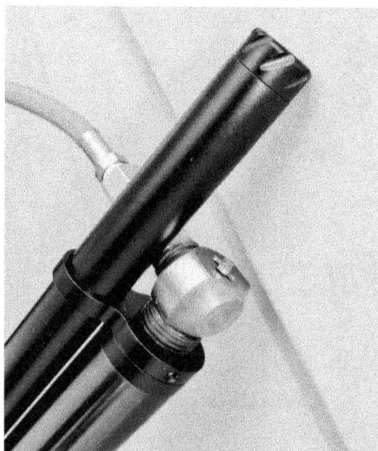

Fill adapter secured to the gun and high-pressure air hose, which leads to a yoke assembly.

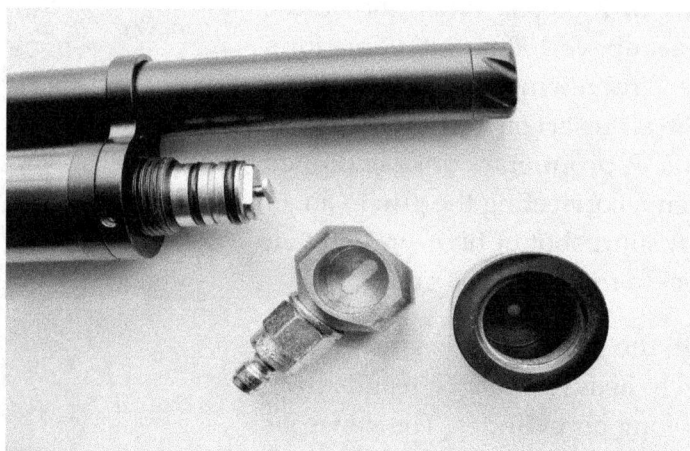

Air Arms collar-type brass fill adapter. The Foster tip snaps into a female hose receptacle. These parts must be HPA rated to prevent bursting!

Yoke & hose assembly: The yoke is a manifold that connects a scuba tank to the high-pressure air (HPA) hose. It clamps on the "K-valve" stem of a standard scuba tank. Just slip the yoke over the K-valve and secure it with a thumbscrew. The screw has a point that locks into an indent on the back of the K-valve. An orifice in the yoke will then align to accept the tank's air supply. The actual yoke should have several threaded ports for the HPA hose, a pressure gauge, and bleeder valve.

My yoke has a small side-mounted pressure gauge, and a foot-long HPA hose section. The gun end of the hose has the QD female fitting that accepts the fill adapter. The yoke housing also has a small bleeder valve, which is needed to vent off excess hose pressure before being disconnected from the gun (it'll rush out with an audible hiss). The whole assembly cost around $90 from a local dive shop. The specialty PCP airgun dealers sell them as complete assembles.

All hooked up and ready to fill. The bleeder valve is closed. The large scuba tank knob can be slowly opened to begin pressurizing the gun.

The yoke clamps to the K-valve of a scuba tank, using the silver-colored knurled knob. Its pointed tip engages a corresponding indent on the rear of the K-valve. Note the hydro-inspection label affixed to the tank.

Once the gun has been pressurized the scuba valve is closed. Residual hose pressure must be relieved prior to disconnection. Cracking the bleed valve will vent it.

Scuba tank: I bought a used aluminum unit from the same shop for $125. I brought the gun along so they could see how it worked. We also made sure the tank had a recent hydro inspection, which must occur every five years. Scuba tanks come in several sizes and materials, but mine is a standard 80 cubic foot aluminum type. Besides being big, it's pretty heavy. It serves as a base station. On a positive note, fills only cost a few dollars and, at 3000 psi, each one provides plenty of shooting. Later, I picked up a second used tank. As one runs low, it's easy enough to top off the gun by switching tanks.

The yoke-mounted pressure gauge indicates just below 2500 psi, safely under the gun's 2900 psi maximum. Rely on this gauge instead of the gun's manometer.

After hose pressure is relieved the fill adapter can be carefully removed from the gun. Reinstall its protective cap and you're ready for action.

Anyone buying a used aluminum tank should look for one made after 1990. Supposedly, earlier models were made from a different alloy. As they age, stress cracks can develop in the neck area. All tanks require periodic inspections. A detailed hydrostatic test must occur every five years, and an internal visual inspection is necessary annually.

For those with deeper pockets, the new high-pressure carbon fiber tanks are not only lighter, but will also handle 4500 psi. Smaller sizes are available, and they make a much better mobile choice. My aluminum tank only travels to and from a dive shop. The more compact CF types are still too big to be carried on foot, but can easily be placed in vehicles or set up at a range. Not every shop can fill one to the 4500 psi pressure, though, so check before you buy! My local shop can't fill to this pressure, which is why I bought a second aluminum model.

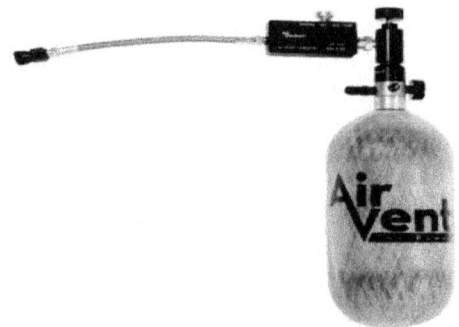

Complete carbon-fiber 90 cubic-inch, 4500 psi system available from Pyramyd Air.

Complete ready-to-use systems: Pyramyd Air lists a 90 CI, 4500 psi carbon fiber tank and hose assembly, ready to use. It's lighter and more compact, but won't sacrifice fills at its rated capacity. Cost runs from $450 - $500.

Pump: Stay tuned. We'll come back to this alternative in a bit.

HOW IT ALL WORKS

A new PCP gun may ship with either no pressure inside, or just a partial charge. You'll need to read its manual in order to properly fill it. Since this process normally occurs near the muzzle end, it's worth checking to make sure the bore is clear. A careful pass with a rod will verify that. Make sure the gun is on "safe". With the necessary fill equipment on hand, you'll need a convenient spot to hook everything up. I can fill my gun with the tank and rifle standing upright, but some systems work better if laid out horizontally.

Step #1: The hose and yoke assembly should be securely attached to the pressurized scuba tank. The bleeder valve will need to in its closed position.

Step #2: The protective cap will need to be removed from the gun's air fitting (or, it may just be a plug-in type).The fill adapter can then be connected to the gun. Make sure the fill adapter is properly attached.

Step #3: At that point you can *slowly* crack the main knob on the scuba tank, while watching the pressure gauge on the yoke (not the gun). Proceed cautiously so maximum pressure isn't exceeded.

A plastic bag offers good insurance against introduction of debris when charging a gun.

Step #4: Shut off the main knob and watch the pressure gauge. Once the correct reading is reached, shut off the tank. Then open the bleeder valve to vent off remaining high-pressure air in the hose. Don't forget this step!

Step #5: Unhook the fill adapter and replace any protective cap. You're done!

The process takes longer to explain than it does to accomplish. It's actually pretty simple. I leave my yoke assembly connected to the scuba tank and cover the hose end with a plastic bag. The actual fill is accomplished in a couple of short stages to minimize heat buildup. A large gush of air will quickly warm the air and gun, creating increased pressure. A 200 bar reading may subside when everything cools. By filling more slowly, the final reading will remain constant. The gun's manometer may vary a bit, or take a little longer to catch up. Not every PCP gun has one, and many that do have small graduations. The gauge on the yoke is a better bet.

At some point, your scuba tank will lose enough pressure to prevent complete fills. It's then time for a trip to a dive shop – unless you have another tank, or a pump.

Pump alternative: You can buy a special high-pressure airgun pump, which will probably come with a HPA hose, air gauge, moisture filter, and bleeder valve. It will superficially resemble a bicycle pump, but it can develop enough extra pressure to blow your Schwinn into orbit.

Another PCP fill option: The Hill HPA pump features a moisture trap

I used a borrowed pump to fill a compact Falcon rifle, and even though the rifle's air cylinder was small, it still required lots of strokes. Starting from zero pressure required a couple hundred. After that, it took around two pumps per shot to replenish the gun. Since the now obsolete Falcon only delivered 25 useful shots, a recharge wasn't *too* demanding. Much like the rhythm involved with a multi-stroke pneumatic, things go much easier after the right technique is mastered. By bending at the knees, body weight can help exert the requisite downward force. If nothing else, you can claim you did your aerobics for the day.

I may yet buy a pump, mainly to throw in the truck during critter control operations. It would also provide some extra insurance. The one made by Hill looks like a winner. It comes with a moisture-trapping "dry-pack" system and pressure gauge. Cost as of 12/14 was $280 from Pomona Airguns.

A system to effectively filter out moisture seems highly worthwhile. The pressure tubes on airguns are made from steel, posing concerns about moisture. Dive shop air is bone dry, so that problem is solved. One possible compromise charging method involves both air sources. When the scuba tank lacks adequate pressure to fully charge the gun, it can be topped off with a pump.

What about a compressor? Much like a plain old bicycle pump, any standard compressor is out. Those with a serious addiction could either join Airguns Anonymous or buy a JRII-PB Electric 4500 psi Pump. The latter option will set you back around $4,200.

WORTH THE EFFORT?

So, who would want a PCP gun in light of all this paraphernalia? For starters, me! I'll go out on a limb and list my Air Arms M-400 as one of a few very favorite rifles. After shooting it, our lead instructor, Mike, soon had his own en route. He bought a lightweight carbon fiber tank to fill it, which is much more portable than my beater aluminum units. This is the system that goes in a truck during pest bird control projects.

We've made some unbelievable shots on crows with these guns, and pigeons don't stand a chance. The rifles are so quiet that many prospective targets won't depart after a shot. Add the possibility of some discreet, scaled precision rifle practice, and you'll really have something. I installed QD sling studs on my rifle so I could mount a Harris bipod. Plopping down into prone beside the house, paintballs on golf tees make great 40-yard targets. The skills necessary for regular hits can be extended to 100-yard golf ball shots later, using a centerfire tactical rifle. Because it's recoilless, a PCP works perfectly off the bipod. Operation from prone is also easy. The same cannot be said of a springer. This performance comes with a price beyond the money aspect. The extra equipment and dependence on an air source are legitimate concerns.

TOP PCP PICKS

Assuming you're willing to make the jump, it's time to narrow down a few PCP choices. The field isn't nearly as crowded as the springer market, but it is getting a bit more crowded. There are some absolutely fantastic rifles available from England, Sweden, and Germany. More recently, some Turkish-built imports have appeared, as well as a few domestic guns.

Up until the last few years anyone shopping for a pre-charged gun would have had to do some serious research. The final choice would have been an exotic import, and few prospective buyers would have had an opportunity to lay their hands on any type of PCP rifle, first. Happily, this situation has changed. One very familiar brand has made significant PCP inroads with a line of interesting pre-charged choices.

Benjamin's .22 Marauder PCP Rifle: I don't own one, but a friend does. He has used it for a couple of years without any difficulties. We shot it beside my Air Arms M-400, which wasn't a fair test considering the price difference. Although I'm very glad to own my British marvel, if the Marauder was available at the time, I probably would've bought it instead. The Benjamin is bigger and less elegant, but not without its own charm. It looks good and is well laid out. One thing I liked was the sling-swivel studs. They were absent on my pricey Air Arms. Although the Benjamin was big, it was comfortable on the shoulder. The safety was located inside the forward part of the trigger guard for ambidextrous access. The grooved receiver made scope mounting easy, and without recoil, choosing the right one became a whole lot simpler. A scope is required, since no sights are supplied.

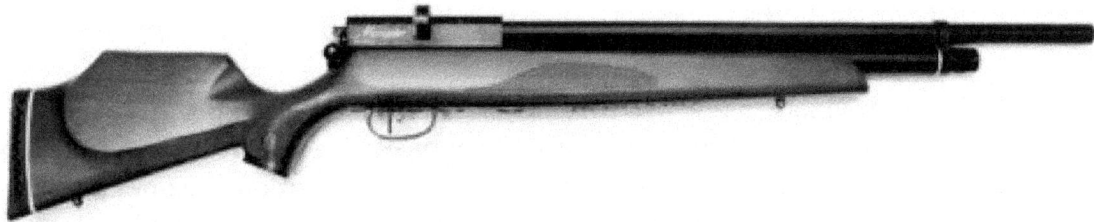

Benjamin's first generation Marauder PCP rifle.

Benjamin's Marauder undergoing accuracy testing. Note the solid sand-bag contact possible due to recoilless shooting.

The Marauder is also a repeater, feeding from a small 10-shot revolving magazine. Each bolt stroke will cycle the magazine and load a new pellet. This feature should be especially appreciated in cold weather. In fact, any time speed is required, loading single pellets directly into the breech can be difficult. A magazine-fed gun takes care of that problem, and extras are available for $15 each.

At 50 yards, 5-shot groups ran slightly more than an inch from my friend's Marauder: perfectly useable accuracy. Thanks to a shrouded barrel, the rifle was fairly quiet, although it had a metallic 'ping". Velocity was less than advertised, but still launched .22 JSB 16 grain pellets at 860 fps. The power can be adjusted via a regulating screw, and a pressure gauge is located in the stock. We got around 25 useful shots from one charge of air on maximum power. The gun's air capacity is listed as 215 CCs. Removing the threaded cap on the muzzle end of the pressure tube reveals a male Foster air fitting, which can be easily connected to the adapter.

Benjamin's latest Marauder offers several internal and external improvements.

More recently, Benjamin has made a few improvements to the Marauder. They tweaked the striker and valve. The former ping is now absent and the shot count has been increased. A .22 caliber rifle should get at least 30 useful shots from a single charge of air. If two extra magazines are purchased, the capacity of all three should cover any normal field outing while serving as a handy fill indicator. The bolt handle is reversible for left-handed shooters. The most obvious change is a new and somewhat lighter black synthetic stock with an adjustable cheek piece. This feature, combined with a grooved receiver, should make scope mounting a breeze. A rubber butt pad won't reduce recoil, because there isn't any! It will support a solid gun mount, and provide traction if the rifle is stored upright.

The Marauder is available in three good calibers: .177, 22, and .25. The latter would be a great pick for anyone after larger prey. Supposedly, the larger bore does generate a bit more noise. Shot count per charge will also be much less – running under 20. For a one airgun owner, the .22 version makes the most sense. Better stock up on lots of pellets, though! With a repeating air rifle, it's awfully easy to go through them.

One thing I've noticed with the few revolving-magazine guns I've shot is that it's fairly easy to double-feed pellets. Normally on such designs, the bolt penetrates the magazine, driving a pellet into the barrel. A lapse of attention may result in a repeat cycle. You can shoot both out, but the process is disconcerting. Supposedly, the Marauder's barrel shroud now contains a few baffles to help reduce noise. It's possible that a double pellet discharge might strike a baffle, causing damage. The bolt travel on new guns takes a bit to smooth out. If you hit a glitch and rework the bolt, you could wind up with a double load. Maintain concentration and things will be fine. A neat little single-shot tray is also sold.

I don't claim any special expertise with this rifle. From secondhand information, I did hear that some earlier production Marauders had mediocre accuracy. The latest reviews look really encouraging. By purchasing a rifle with a synthetic stock, you'll assured of the latest production. The trigger has been redesigned, and is also adjustable. Benjamin recommends charging the Marauder to slightly lower pressure than its 3000 psi maximum. They claim a 179 bar/2600 psi fill will produce the most consistent velocities for optimum accuracy. It should be fun to experiment. The expectation of very good accuracy seems reasonable, especially considering its retail price. The Marauder is widely distributed, so cost is competitive, running around $500.

The new Marauder Armada Magpul is neither lightweight nor inexpensive, but it should attract the tactical crowd.

Hot off the press is a black rifle version that superficially resembles an AR-15. The "Armada Magpul PCP Rifle" is fitted with a collapsible stock, pistol grip, and free-floated forend that accepts Picatinny rail sections. A large 4-16x50 scope and bipod are included. The heart of this rifle is still a bolt-action Marauder. At over ten pounds, it's no lightweight, nor is it cheap. Cost is $1000.

By comparison, at $500, a regular Marauder is a bargain. Still, it won't work without air, so you'll need one of the following combinations:

Marauder .22 PCP rifle:	$500	Marauder .22 PCP rifle:	$500
Hose & yoke with gauge:	$ 90	Benjamin Pump with hose:	$180
Used scuba tank:	$100	*Includes fill adapter*	—
JSB Jumbo Exact (500)	$ 20	JSB .22Jumbo Exact (500)	$ 20
	$710 + scope		$700 + scope

Note the absence of a scope and rings, which will add at least another $100 to the package price. That's more than double the price of that RWS Model 34. A new scuba tank will tack on another $100. If you can live with more noise, there is a lower-cost PCP option...

Just when you think you've seen it all, along comes Benjamin's 357 Bulldog PCP bull-pup airgun good for about 10 shots, with .380 ACP equivalent power.

Benjamin's Discovery "Dual Fuel" Rifle: This unique little rifle is a no-frills single-shot version of the Marauder with some unique features. Interestingly, it can run off either high-pressure air or carbon dioxide gas. Using a supplied "degasser" tool, a valve in the rear of the gun can be gradually cracked to bleed off all onboard pressure. Or, with patience, you can just shoot off the pressure instead. At that point, the pressure cylinder can be refilled with either HPA or bulk-fill CO2. Compressed air will provide the highest velocity, and carbon dioxide will yield the most shots.

In PCP mode, muzzle velocity runs around 800 fps with standard weight .22 pellets. That's a very useful velocity that should cover most bases. Unlike most other PCP rifles, the Discovery manages to achieve this performance at significantly lower pressure.

You'll get a whole lot of extra shots with carbon dioxide, but they'll be at lower velocity. Some die-hard paintball gamers have their own fill station on hand, in which case a Discovery is logical choice. Pyramyd Air also sells a refillable 20-ounce CO2 tank for around $26. Many sporting goods stores sell paintball equipment, and are equipped to fill these tanks. A separate CO2 fill connection is also required, and the cost is around $36. The whole concept is similar to HPA technology, but it won't interchange. A cylindrical coupling is screwed to the CO2 tank with hand pressure. It has a short hose with a fill adapter that connects to the gun. Inverting the tank will allow CO2 to top off the gun at its 900 psi operating pressure. After that, you should be good for around 60 shots, depending on the temperature. Several hundred shots may be possible from a 20-ounce tank, making this system an economical alternative to 12-gram disposable cartridges. Velocity should be adequate for target practice, running somewhere around 600 fps.

Benjamin's innovative Discovery Dual Fuel rifle, complete with a pump.

Most people will probably use high-pressure air. The Marauder's scuba-charged technology will work, but the plain Jane, lower pressure Discovery seems like a great candidate for a hand pump. The gun runs off only 2000 psi – one third less than most other PCP rifles. Its air 135 cc reservoir is smaller, too. Nevertheless, the Discovery can deliver around 25 useful shots at 800 fps, or even a bit more. That's my preferred hunting threshold, which equals 20 ft·lbs - enough energy to anchor squirrel-sized game within 35 yards.

A set of fiber-optic open sights are standard, and the receiver is grooved for tip-off scope rings. The trigger is non-adjustable, but acceptable. Accuracy is reportedly quite good, and the gun has enough range to justify an optical sighting system. A small 4X one-inch rimfire scope would make a nice addition, and would maintain the rifle's trim lines. Sling studs are absent, but could be easily installed. The stock looks like real walnut. Unlike the Marauder, it lacks any checkering. Somehow, that doesn't detract from the Discovery, which seems somewhat like a throwback to the well-made air rifles from the 1960s. One concession is a plastic trigger guard that houses a push-button safety similar to the Benjamin pump-up guns. The Discovery handles nicely and has relatively small proportions, but it's actually stocked for an adult. It's pretty neat!

Discovery .22 PCP bare rifle:	$260	Discovery .22 PCP rifle package	$400
Hose & yoke with gauge:	$ 90	*(Benjamin Pump with hose & fill*	
Used scuba tank:	$100	*adapter*	—
JSB Express Exact (500)	$ 18	JSB .22 Jumbo Exact (500)	$ 18
	$468 + scope		$418 + scope

You can purchase the Discovery solo, or as a ready-to-shoot package with a Benjamin HPA pump. Not only is the whole setup cheaper than a bare Marauder, but it should also appeal to those seeking true air independence. The degassing tool is extra. One kicker: the Discovery doesn't have a built-in moderator. In other words, it will be pretty loud.

Air Force Talon SS: Another PCP brand worth mentioning is the "Air Force" line. These guns are also U.S.-made, and have interesting design elements. A removable high-pressure air bottle serves as the stock, and the gun is laid out as an inline platform. All are single-shots with easy breech access that permits the use of nearly any projectile. A bolt runs the action, but it's a slightly unconventional design. When opened, its large handle points straight up, underneath the scope base. Plenty of clearance is provided for its operation. To load a pellet, the bolt is rotated either left or right until upright. At that point, it will slide forward on a sleeve to expose the barrel breech. A safety inside the trigger guard will then automatically engage. After inserting a pellet, the bolt is drawn rearward and locked downward. The overall gun design permits ambidextrous use, and a butt plate attaches to the rear of the air bottle for a comfortable gun mount.

The Air Force guns look very futuristic, with a pistol grip and elevated scope rail reminiscent of an M16-type carry handle. Models are available with built-in sound moderators, and guns are offered in all four popular calibers. There are so many choices that picking a winner is tough. It really just boils down to personal preference.

One grabber is the "Escape SS". It's very compact and powerful, but employs a shrouded barrel for quiet shooting. It should appeal to many survivalists, but its extra punch requires more air consumption, which cuts down on useful shots.

The futuristic Air Force Talon PCP rifle is a real grabber with a number of interesting features.

The .22 Talon SS may be a better compromise. Its 490 cc air supply is generous and, if more is required, a spare bottle could be tucked in a day pack. The barrel is shrouded for relatively quiet shooting. Since its power is adjustable, velocity can be dialed down for increased stealth and extra shots. With the right scope, trajectory could be compensated for as well. Weight is only 5 ¼ lbs, and the Talon's design results in a very compact rifle, less than 33 inches long. By removing the air bottle, the gun will become even shorter and well-suited for discreet carrying or storage.

The Talon's air bottle can be charged while connected to the gun, or when it's removed. The former method looks easier because a fitting on the gun permits easy attachment of a fill adapter. At that point, a fill is the same as any other PCP gun. Exchanging bottles with the Talon's "Spin-Loc" looks a bit more complicated, requiring a spanner wrench to tighten up a sleeve. Still, it would make a nice option for extended field use. A pressure gauge on the gun indicates the amount of air in a bottle. Some people claim it can be off a bit, but at some point, shooters will learn their useable shot count and then do a refill.

Velocity can be adjusted with a rotating drum, using just fingers. A graduated scale indicates its setting. The numbers don't correlate exactly to velocity, so some experimentation will be necessary. A chronograph is the best way to figure this out. The Talon SS has a short 12-inch barrel, housed inside a shroud. On its highest setting, more air is expelled than can actually be used. A 24-inch accessory barrel will make full use of maximum pressure, but it will extend beyond the moderator. The standard SS length is a practical choice. On a medium setting, the shrouded barrel will still produce decent velocity and a quiet report. Shot count will vary with power adjustments. The relatively large HPA bottle should provide up to 60 small game shots, or as many as 200 plinking shots on the lowest settings.

By most accounts, filling the large air bottle is a real workout with a pump. It'll take a pounding, so a good one will be necessary. The "Hill" is touted as a quality choice. A scuba tank solves this issue, but it will yield less fills than other PCP designs. The Talon's 490 cc bottle seems like a great candidate for both options. As pressure in the scuba tank subsides, a pump could be used to top off the bottle. There's also a third option…

Because it runs off bottles, CO2 becomes another choice. A simple adapter is all that is needed. It connects a CO2 bottle to the gun, and the needed valve adjustments are built into this part. It'll run off 12 or 20-ounce paintball bottles, producing many more shots than HPA would allow. Velocity will be lower, running somewhere around 600 fps with .22 standard pellets. As noted previously, cold weather and CO2 don't mix. Below 50 degrees, performance will suffer greatly.

The Talon comes without swivel studs, but an accessory set is offered that will attach without gunsmithing. Most shooters will go for a scope, although a set of fiber-optic sights is also sold. They're very high to properly accommodate the Air Force design. The scope base is a grooved type, and a set of very high rings will be needed by most shooters. It's a similar situation to an AR-15, complete with greater bore to scope offset. In the case of an Air Force gun, the difference will be close to four inches. That's quite a bit! In an upcoming chapter, methods will be shown to plot the steeper trajectories of airgun pellets. This information will prove useful when small targets are involved at different ranges. The greater sight offset of a Talon will require extra allowances. Rifle canting will be another concern, causing misses at greater ranges. Maintaining level crosshairs helps to overcome the problem.

I'd personally go for a more conventional design that locates a scope closer to the bore, but many people will no doubt be struck by the racy Air Force guns. By most accounts, they shoot very well. The compact and versatile Talon SS remains a viable choice. There are so many models that the whole Air Force line is worth a look.

Pre-charged .22 airgun picks							
Make	**Model**	**Weight**	**MV**	**CC**	**Shroud**	**Repeater**	**Price**
Benjamin	Marauder	7.3 lbs	900	215	Yes	Yes	$500
Benjamin	Discovery	5.2 lbs	800	135	No	No	$260
Air Force	Talon SS	5.3 lbs	800	490	Yes	No	$590
Benjamin	M-Pistol *	2.7 lbs	700	65	Yes	Yes	$400
Includes shoulder stock							

A la carte - Benjamin's Marauder Pistol: Air pistols were briefly addressed in a previous chapter with this comment: "Unless you're looking strictly for a trainer, I'd skip an air pistol. Most just don't develop enough power to be useful in the field – especially for survival purposes. Some are on the edge, but they are just plain big."

Benjamin's Marauder 8-shot PCP pistol provides decent velocity and a useful shot count.

Another problem is that many people don't shoot a handgun very well. For those that can drive tacks, Benjamin's .22 PCP pistol may have value. The trouble is, it's just too big to carry in any kind of normal concealed fashion. A holster is almost certainly out, but a Marauder pistol would fit in a briefcase or pack. For *all* shooters, a compromise solution exists: we can turn this handgun into a very compact carbine. It comes with a skeleton shoulder stock that will interchange with the grip panels. This transformation would be a violation of the National Firearms Act if the 12-inch-barreled Marauder fired conventional ammunition, but of course it doesn't. The result is an NFA-legal, short-barreled gun with adequate power for close-range use.

Adding the shoulder stock transforms the pistol into a handy PCP carbine.

The Marauder pistol is very much like its larger and previously detailed cousin. Both are bolt-action repeaters, but the pistol feeds from a slightly smaller and non-interchangeable 8-shot magazine. The air reservoir is smaller too, which limits useful shots. Still, the pistol manages to deliver roughly 25 consistent pellets at around 700 fps. This velocity is very similar to many spring-powered air rifles. A shrouded barrel keeps it as quiet and, with its shoulder stock attached, the PCP pistol is much more compact. The recoilless design also eliminates the need for special shooting techniques or airgun-rated scopes. Since it ships without sights, some sort of optical system will be necessary. Fortunately, the receiver is grooved.

The shoulder stock can be mounted, using the same pair of screws that secure the pistol's grip panels. If both configurations have appeal, choosing a useful aiming device can pose a challenge. Pistol scopes have much longer eye relief, needed to accommodate extended arms. They won't allow a full field of view when mounted to the receiver of a rifle. The same problem happens in reverse when mounting rifle scopes on handguns. What to do? How about a dot sight?

B-Square sells adapter bases that slip over the grooves of rimfire receivers. Once secured with clamping screws, they'll permit mounting of Weaver-type scope rings. Most dot sights are designed to match a Weaver base, and the smallest types should work with just one B-Square adapter.

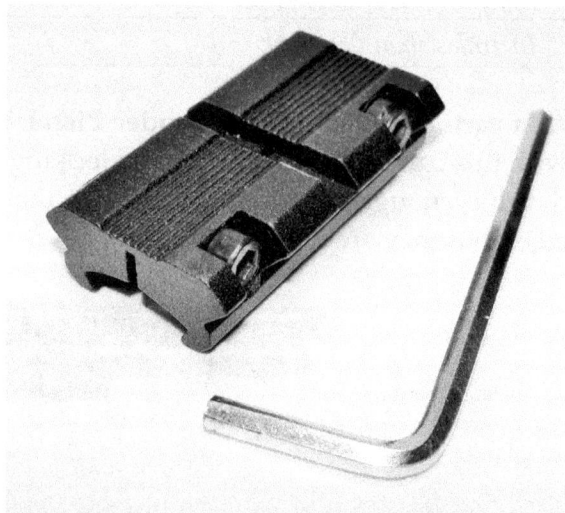

The B-Square adapter clamps to a grooved receiver and accepts Weaver-type mounts.

I have a spare Burris Fast-Fire, so I tried it on a B-Square base section. As expected, the sight didn't quite fit. The Fast-Fire has interchangeable bases, and mine is equipped with a Picatinny type. It will also clamp on a Weaver TO-10 grooved receiver to Weaver adapter base. You *might* be able to slip a TO-10 over the grooves on the Marauder's receiver. I'd want to try that at a gun shop. The TO-10 is a long one-piece base, secured with a couple of pointed set screws. If it will go on, this base will need to sit forward of the magazine.

The cross-slots on the Weaver base are about .015" wider than the B-Square's (both depths are the same). The cross-bolt on the Fast-Fire sight won't quite seat in the narrower B-Square cut. I've run into this before. With patience and a small file, it's easy to widen the cut in the soft aluminum base. Afterwards, you can dab the bare metal with a permanent black marking pen. It's a bit of a hassle, but the B-Square adapter base tightens with a pair of side screws. Unlike a set screw type, it won't leave any permanent indentations in a gun. A Fast-Fire only needs one of the two base sections, so you should be able to mount it ahead of or behind the magazine. The result would be an ultra-compact aiming arrangement, without any eye relief limitations. Access to the magazine would also be unimpeded.

There are a number of similar small sights on the market. You might even find one that will properly nest into a B-Square adapter's cross slots. If you can track down something that will clamp directly to the Marauder's receiver, life will be even simpler. A tube-type dot sight with tip-off rings will easily do that, at the expense of a somewhat larger and taller assembly. Since the supplied shoulder stock has some drop, the lowest workable sighting arrangement will be appreciated.

The same dot sight should work equally well in pistol mode. In fact, I really like a dot sight on a handgun. It provides intuitive aiming, and really shrinks my groups. A dot lacks the fine precision of a true scope, but should still be useful within the limits of a 700 fps carbine. A finer 2-MOA (minute-of-angle) dot would be the better bet.

The Burris Fast-Fire is an ultra-compact electronic dot-sight that doesn't spoil the lines of a handgun or carbine.

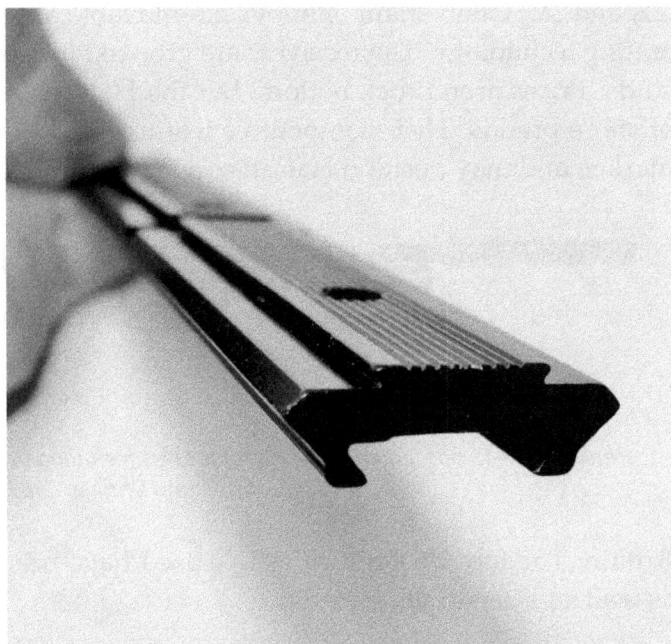

Another possible optics mounting option: Weaver's T-10 base slips over a grooved receiver and is secured with set-screws.

As a carbine, this rig would be a *very* compact package. Out to 30 yards, it should have enough punch for use on pigeons or squirrels. This performance is analogous to that of most spring rifles, so the biggest drawback may be the pistol's limited air supply. A big plus is that it could be more easily charged with a hand pump than any standard rifle.

OTHER PCP RIFLES

While the U.S. airgun market has been flooded with a torrent of imported barrel-cocking springers, until recently, the PCP import stream was really just a trickle. The flow has since increased, and although the initial British and European manufacturers remain in the game, others have jumped in. The increased supply of PCP guns is at least partially attributable to modern Eurasian gun-making capabilities.

Turkey: A relative newcomer to the U.S. is Hatsan. They offer an interesting line of Turkish-built PCP rifles that feature synthetic stocks and anti-double-feed repeating bolt-actions. Calibers include .177, .22, and .25. One variant employs a removable air cylinder, and most use some sort of sound-moderating technology. The receivers are grooved for scope rings, and the black plastic stocks have sling studs. Prices aren't rock bottom, but the Hatsans as a whole are more affordable than many other offshore brands. Their competitive features and pricing are already taking a bite out of the import market, and may position Hatsan as a significant U.S. player.

Hatsan's AT44S has a number of neat features including an interchangeable air cylinder, anti-double feed mechanism, and Weaver-type scope mount slots.

Britain: The few UK-built rifles I've used have been real jewels. Their prices match this description as well, at least, to some extent.

At this point, I have enjoyed very positive experiences with three Air Arms PCP rifles. Anyone looking for first class PCP guns should be happy with an Air Arms Model 500 single-shot or 510 repeater. The kicker is, they start at around a thousand bucks, which doesn't include their necessary fill equipment and optics.

Daystate has an even pricier line of elegant British PCP rifles that should please the pickiest shooters. Some run off larger air bottles, and a .30 caliber model is even available. Each is an absolutely stunning air rifle, light years beyond a layman's perception of a common pellet or BB gun.

Other intriguing English PCP rifles are sold by BSA, Webley, and Brocock. While some are priced around the thousand-dollar level, others run a bit cheaper. If you buy a British import, make sure it is an FAC version. Otherwise, you may find yourself with a 12 ft·lb model.

Europe: Perhaps the ultimate refinement of airgun technology can be seen in Anschutz, Feinwerkbau, and Walther match PCP rifles. Their main objective is to place .177 projectiles through one hole during controlled conditions. Anyone intrigued by accuracy and precision should window shop these rifles, strictly out of curiosity. Unfortunately - or maybe fortunately, due to their prices - they won't serve well in the bush.

Gamo's new Coyote PCP rifle joins the affordable pre-charged fray.

On the other hand, the PCP rifles from Cometa, Dianna, HW, and FX will cover all bases. Like the British guns, these are handsome and well-built rifles with similar pricing. The FX Independence is perhaps the ultimate choice. It merges the benefits of a pre-charged rifle with those of a multi-stroke design. The Independence can be shot normally in PCP mode, or it can be topped off between shots with a pumping lever. Only three strokes per shot will maintain its pressure. Weight isn't excessive, but its $1800 sticker may be a greater burden. Another innovative design is the FX Verminator Extreme, which shoots arrows as well as pellets. Sold in a compact take-down case, it comes with two quick-change barrels and two scopes mounted in QD rings. A supplied crossbow scope is used with arrows which slip over the thin archery barrel. Rather than very short crossbow bolts, it shoots conventional arrows approaching compound bow velocities of around 270 – 290 fps. The gun runs off a detachable HPA bottle that yields plenty of shots. This survival-oriented versatility comes at a steeper price of $2500. Airguns of Arizona has an interesting video on their web-site.

Hot off the press is a new PCP rifle from Gamo. Their new "Coyote" is a repeater with an action that strongly resembles the British BSA. Since Gamo owns both brands, this is understandable. Cost is fairly reasonable at around $500.

Asia: Some unusual Korean pre-charged guns are made by Eun Jin, and Sam Yang; the latter catering to a big bore market with .357, .45, and .50 caliber PCP rifles. The Evanix guns are more conventional, rivaling those from Europe or the UK, at a slightly lower cost.

*How about a .50-caliber pre-charged air rifle? The Korean-built Sam Yang
Dragonclaw is just such a gun.*

FINAL PCP THOUGHTS

These guns run off high-pressure air that will quickly escape if not properly contained. Considerable engineering goes into a pre-charged design, which relies heavily on well-fitted O-rings. These small seals won't last forever, so the likelihood of failure increases without periodic replacement. My Air Arms rifle is a well-built machine, but after a decade of service, it's going back to Pomona Airguns for an overhaul. Although I'm very comfortable with firearms, the complex internals of a pneumatic gun deserve the services of a well-equipped professional. The slightest nick or speck of dirt will cause a leak, and parts don't grow on trees. You won't find an airgunsmith on every corner, so shipping and turnaround time are concerns. You could expect a lower-cost gun to need work more often, which is something to consider before buying any PCP gun. If it leaks when you need it the most, you may be up that bad-smelling creek without a paddle. In that case, a springer will have sudden appeal.

A pre-charged pneumatic is one heck of an airgun, but it's not for everyone. The best way to get a handle on the whole PCP field is to reserve time for a fascinating Internet session. But remember, you can mail-order an airgun. Better lock up your credit cards first!

Another big-bore contender is the new and futuristic Evanix Max, which is also available in conventional airgun calibers.

CHAPTER 8

AIRGUN SIGHTS AND SCOPES

As we've seen, there are a number of airgun choices capable of harvesting small game at surprising distances. But lacking the greater power of firearms, shot placement is critical. The accuracy is certainly there, but exact placement of pellets will require a precision aiming system. For many of us, that means a telescopic sight, more commonly referred to as a scope. As we'll soon see, not just any type will work, or even survive, the unique dynamics of many airguns. Scope mounts are a related concern. The inherent limitations imposed by some airgun designs may limit our choices, and some people may be better off without any type of scope. Those looking for more detailed information about sights, scopes, and mounts may wish to consult *Rimfire Rifles: A Buyer's and Shooter's Guide.*

OPEN SIGHTS

Casual airgun shooters or those with good eyes may do alright with the sights that come standard on many spring guns. There's a reason open sights are often included on barrel-cocking rifles: droop. Mounting both sights directly to the barrel solves this mechanical misalignment problem. Lately, fiber-optic sights have become popular. They are a whole lot easier to see, and their large adjustment knobs make zeroing an easy and tool-free process. Iron (or open) sights won't provide the degree of precision needed to engage very small targets at other than very close range. Any serious accuracy testing is also out, but won't matter much within the practical limits of open sights. You could easily plink cans at 25 to 40 yards, but paintballs on golf tees won't be hit too often. The pump-up crowd will likely stick with their factory-issued open sights, due to the inherent difficulties of mounting a scope. For everyone, a receiver (or peep) sight may be an option.

These open sights have fiber-optic elements and are factory-issue from RWS.

RECEIVER SIGHTS

This aiming system has some benefits, two be-ing simplicity and cost. A peep, or aperture sighting system, is also more precise than open sights. We might consider this aiming system as a bridge between open sights and scopes. Back when my eyes were younger, I tried a Williams unit designed for rimfire grooved receivers. It clamped right onto the scope grooves of a Beeman .20 R-1 springer, and sighted in without difficulty. That may have involved a bit of luck, since a receiver sight is usually higher than an open rear blade. Sometimes a higher front sight will be needed, but in this case, the large German-built facto-ry sights were tall enough for the necessary elevation. I unscrewed the barrel-mounted rear sight assembly and gained a streamlined and handy package. A better choice for many would be the Williams aperture sight market-

Peep sight alignment: It's an affordable, fast and intuitive system.

ed for springers. The different Benjamin M-392/Williams setup would provide the same benefits to multi-stroke pneumatic shooters. Those with more sophisticated rifles will be looking towards optics.

SCOPES

Again, *Rimfire Rifles: A Buyer's and Shooter's Guide* is a good source for general scope information, as well as mounting tips. Most of it is applicable to airguns as well. Rather than rehash it all here, let's look at a few airgun-specific concerns.

First off, spring gun shooters will need to choose an airgun-rated scope. There are plenty of airgun scopes to sift through. The trick is in finding one that will maintain zero and survive the vibrations of a spring or gas piston rifle. The better types use industrial adhesives to double-brace all internal components against severe, reverse recoil. Such construction won't be a concern for any pre-charged pneumatic owners whose systems are recoilless. A decent rimfire scope will serve nicely, although in actuality, many are designed for either system.

The numbers: A 3-9x40 scope is one with an adjustable magnification from 3 to 9 power. Its front (objective) bell is about 40 mm in diameter. Not too coincidentally, that's more than enough for most airgun uses, which happen at relatively close distances. Too much magnification results in reduced field of view, which is area visible within the scope. If cranked up to 9 power, a 15-yard target might be difficult to locate. The fix is to use it on a lower setting. I'm completely happy with a 4 or 6 power scope for airgun use. A 2x7 variable is another good choice, and a 3x9 will work. I do own a couple of others with more magnification, but I bought them primarily for other features not available in lower-power scopes. Inexpensive variables may cause projectile group shifts as their magnifications are adjusted. It's worth checking for that by shooting groups at several settings.

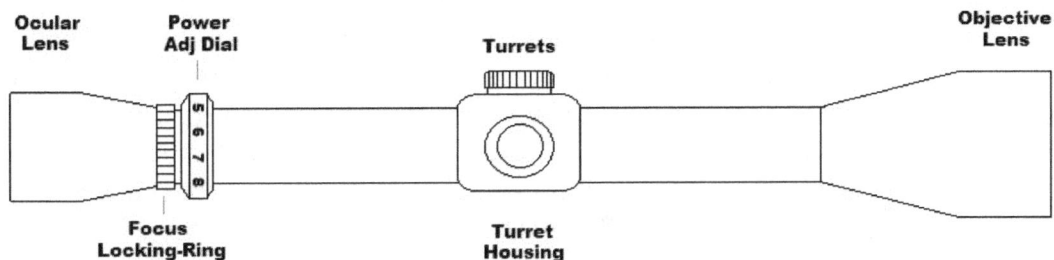

Scope nomenclature: The front end of an airgun scope will often have an adjustable-objective lens for close-range focus.

This Hawke 3-9 x 40 AO airgun scope is plenty of glass. The "AO" stands for "adjustable objective", which permits close-range parallax correction.

Eye relief: This is the distance from the rear of a scope to the shooter's eye, where a proper image can be acquired. With most scopes, it'll be roughly around 3 inches. I always look for a bit more, which helps during some mounting situations. Some, like the Burris Timberline, provide up to five inches, which is quite a bit. If the eye isn't located within a scope's eye relief range, an incomplete image will result, so generous numbers can be good.

This Bushnell 4x12 has an adjustable-objective suitable for airgun use. The parallax setting is dialed to 30 yards.

Parallax: One potential problem for rimfire and airgun shooters involves a condition whereby the image and the crosshairs diverge. The resulting internal misalignment can cause shot group shifts without perfectly centered eye placement. The reticle (crosshairs) and image will only coincide at one distance, so most centerfire scopes are parallax-corrected for 100 or 150 yards. If you aim at a close target, don't be surprised to see the crosshairs wander as your head shifts position. This effect can be especially pronounced at short rimfire and airgun ranges. The reticle and target will be on different planes, and you'll be experiencing parallax. A parallax-adjustable (P/A) scope is therefore worthwhile. Most airgun shots will likely occur inside 50 yards, and some may be much closer. Especially for indoor use at short ranges, the ability to parallax-correct a scope will be appreciated. The true airgun types can be adjusted down to 10 yards or less, whereas many centerfire varmint models stop at 50 yards.

Many P/A scopes employ a rotating front bell (objective lens) which is twisted until a small witness mark on the scope's tube coincides with the appropriate distance setting. You'll sometimes see them referred to as AO models, which stands for "adjustable objective". Lately, side-mounted parallax adjustment models have become popular. The P/A knob is located on the turret housing, opposite the windage dial. Fine tuning is thus more convenient, especially from prone. Regardless of the design, in theory, the graduations will reflect the actual yardage to eliminate parallax. Unfortunately, this is not always the case, especially with lower-priced scopes.

Side-mounted adjustable parallax systems are becoming increasingly popular. They're much easier to use from prone or off a bench.

Turrets: We need the means to adjust our scope so that projectiles impact where intended. Many conventional hunting scopes have smaller elevation and windage knobs, protected by threaded caps. Once removed, a series of graduations permit incremental adjustments through a scaled system of clicks. For example, four clicks might equal a crosshair adjustment of one inch at 100 yards (or ¼ inch at 25 yards). Turrets are also sometimes marked in MOA increments. Fortunately, we can keep things fairly simple. As it turns out 1 MOA equals roughly 1 inch at 100 yards (1.047 to be exact). If your turrets are graduated in ¼ MOA increments, 4 clicks should equate to a reticle adjustment of 1 inch at 100 yards. As long as you can reference everything from that distance, it's easy to extrapolate other ranges. One MOA equals ½ inch at 50 yards or ¼ inch at 25 yards. Once each knob (or turret) is properly adjusted, our rifle is "sighted in" or "zeroed" for a specific distance determined by the shooter. At that point, the capped designs are generally left alone.

Typical field turret system with ¼ MOA graduated clicks.

However, target or ballistic-compensating turrets are now the rage. They work in a similar manner, but the turrets are large, raised affairs that display micrometer-like graduations. Shooters dial on the requisite number of clicks for a predetermined yardage and aim dead on. Some are even designed for specific calibers and trajectories. In either case, frequent adjustments will occur. That's fine and dandy, so long as the scope's internals are built well enough for repeatable results. The trouble is, many of the cheaper versions aren't.

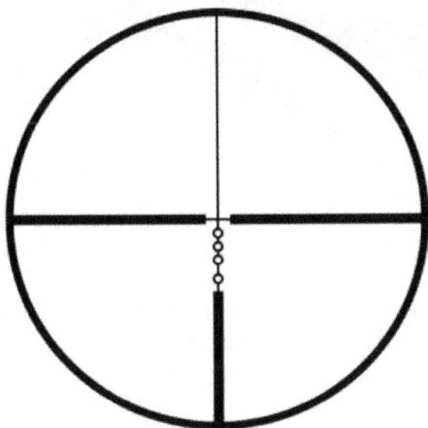

A ballistic-aiming reticle like the Nikon system employs multiple aiming points for different ranges.

Each graduation on these target turrets equals ¼ MOA. The longer marks indicate one MOA values. A set-screw allows the scale to be set to "0" after sighting in.

Reticles: This term refers to our aiming system, often referred to as "crosshairs". The simplest type is just a sect of thin horizontal and vertical bisecting wires. The "duplex" version has thicker outer sections that help center the image. But, lately, ballistic aiming reticles have caught on. Burris popularized this design with their "Ballistic-Plex" system, which has a small series of tick marks on the lower crosshair section. Spaced out in trajectory-equivalent intervals, the marks can be used as holdover aiming spots to compensate for drop. Other firms like Nikon use circles. The options among all manufacturers continue to grow. Mil-dots are another big seller, especially with the long range tactical crowd. The crosshairs display a series of dots, which can be used to estimate range, as well as for holdover.

Level crosshairs are necessary with these reticles, in order to prevent windage errors. Also, most will only calibrate with trajectories at maximum magnification. Although designed primarily for long-range shooting measured in hundreds of yards, ballistic reticles can be still be used at airgun distances. In fact, Hawke sells a line of scopes calibrated for this purpose. Other types may work through experimental shooting. The tick marks or dots will coincide with pellet impacts at some point.

Since no turret adjustments are needed, a ballistic reticle is probably a safer bet with less expensive scopes. However, even those shooters with duplex-type reticles needn't feel completely left out. The juncture of the thick/thin bottom crosshair section can often be used as a long range hold point.

Size: For some reason, large scopes are often seen on airguns. Some of this popularity may be attributable to the sport of Field Target, a formal airgun event that simulates small game and varmint hunting. Knock-down metallic silhouettes are located at unknown distances throughout a wooded setting that simulates field conditions. In order to make consistent hits with looping pellet trajectories, shooters must accurately determine each target's distance. As it turns out, fairly precise estimates can be achieved with the right scope. A popular choice is a large one with high magnification and a side-mounted parallax adjustment. Ballistic turrets are the norm, and shooters expend much effort matching their trajectories to the click values of the turrets. Once established, they apply the requisite number of clicks for a given distance, and then aim dead on.

A large scope may interfere with, or even prevent gun operation. This combination works but loading is a bit tricky.

Two key factors are wind and the exact target distance. For all riflemen, wind estimation is as much an art as science. Rangefinders are a vast improvement over distance estimates, but they're not allowed on FT courses. Instead, competitors employ parallax adjustment wheels with circumferences large enough to display homemade yardage scales. On very high scope magnifications, targets will only be in sharp focus at one precise parallax adjustment. The serious shooters spend even more time correlating these adjustments to precise yardages. It takes a giant wheel to record all of the range settings, which results in a very large scope. When mounted to a relatively hefty airgun the final setup will be really big. Within the confines of a small FT area, such a package is bearable, but in real life field conditions, it'll quickly become a burden. A more useful all-around airgun will need a smaller aiming system.

Still, the trend towards large optics persists. The more powerful spring rifles are fairly hefty without any optics, and big scopes add even more weight. Their increased mass can also lead to inertial creep from the recoil of a springer. Those scopes with huge objective bells will need higher rings, which can increase bore offset while degrading a shooter's cheek weld. An overly large model may also interfere with the operation of some rifles. So, despite the numerous examples shown in catalogs, bigger isn't always better. Not only that, but packing all of these features into a low-priced scope means something has got to give.

Quality: As previously noted, the package airguns come with *some* type of scope which may, or may not be mounted. Since most such combinations are intended to meet highly competitive price-points, scope quality can be sketchy. It's hard enough to shake out a dependable barrel-cocking gun from this crowded field, let alone a decent optical sight. That's why I'd rather shop for my own scope. In fact, many package gun purchasers wind up doing the same thing later.

Airguns and scopes bear a logical cost relationship. It just doesn't make much sense to mount a top-dollar scope on an inexpensive gun, but a poorly-built scope is just a waste of money. The RWS M-34 and Beeman R-9 scope combinations are an attempt to match appropriately priced optics to serviceable spring rifles. The pre-charged picks were shown without optics since nearly any type will work.

Springers posed the challenge. I've used these airguns on and off for years, but most of my recent airgun activity has been centered on PCP rifles. Some updated research was necessary. After checking published airgun literature and website threads, several contenders emerged. The scopes that follow should work on all airguns.

Burris: My battle-scarred collection of older Burris Mini-Scopes will survive on anything that shoots. Unfortunately, they have been discontinued. I'd expect the newer Burris "Timberline" scopes to perform equally well, since they share many common features. If you call Burris and ask, they'll tell you that all of their scopes are rated for airguns. The Timberline 4.5-14x32 AO has a bit more magnification than I'd prefer, but its adjustable objective will focus as close as 7 yards. The Ballistic-Plex reticle has holdover lines, which can be useful within airgun ranges. By fiddling with its magnification, the reticle's aiming points will often coincide with pellet impacts at various distances. On maximum magnification, eye relief is touchy, so mine seldom goes above 10X. Size isn't excessive; the scope is only around 11.3 inches long and weighs 15 ounces. I always look for lots of eye relief, due to my build and shooting style. The Timberline has up to five inches – way more than most others. Folks who prefer to mount their scopes far forward *might* have problems with the objective bell overhanging the breech of a barrel-cocking rifle. Cost is around $270, and the "forever warranty" is reassuring.

Burris 4.5-14 x 32 AO Timberline with Ballistic-Plex reticle.

Bushnell: This brand has been around forever and a day. I've used them for decades, and their clear lenses are a given. The cheaper scopes will work on rimfires, but spring gun shooters should move up a notch or two. Plenty of "Banners" are mounted to airguns. A 4-12x40 AO is mounted to my Beeman R-9. It's more glass than I really need, but it came with the rifle. The mounts are a set of rugged 1-inch Sportsmatch rings that clamp securely to the grooved receiver. A stud in the bottom of one ring engages a corresponding stop hole in the rifle for extra anti-creep insurance. For me, the height is perfect on the R-9, and so far, this arrangement is still going strong. The next Bushnell step is the "Trophy" line. The XLT 4-12x40 AO can be had for around $160.

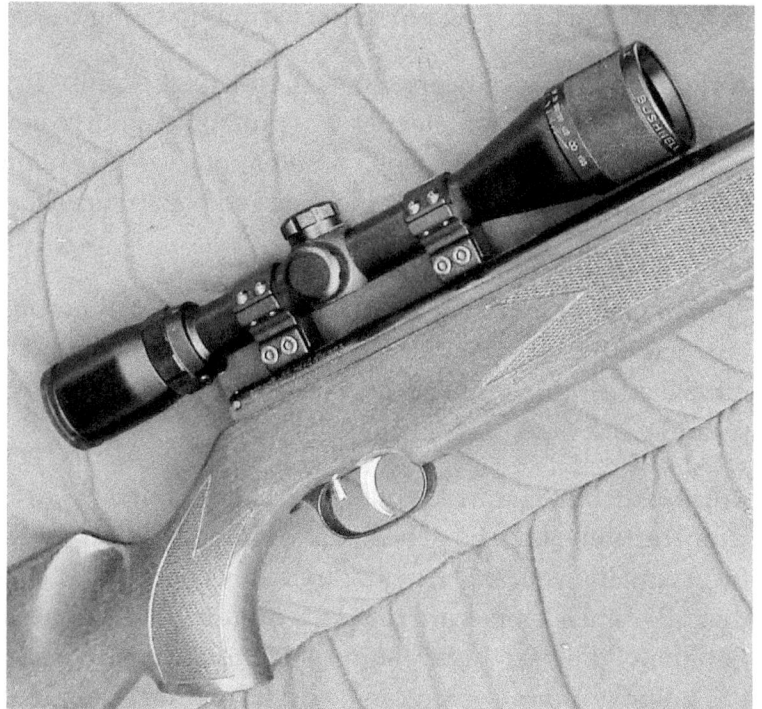

Bushnell 4-12 x 40 AO Banner in 1" Sportsmatch rings, mounted to a Beeman R-9 springer.

Hawke: These scopes have become very popular for use on crossbows and airguns. By accessing their website, you can correlate their aiming reticles to the ballistics of your gun. The Airmax 3-9x40 EV is plenty of glass for a sporting springer, and sells for the reasonable cost of $160. A larger 4x12 version goes for $170. Either would be an equally good choice for a pre-charged rifle.

Hawke's 3-9 x 40 AO Airmax EV is purpose built for airguns, including hard-recoiling springers.

Leupold: Their "Ultra-Light" scopes were formerly sold as "Compacts". The 3-9x33 EFR is made for airguns, as indicated by its "extreme focus range" parallax adjustment. The two I've owned were top-notch scopes with clear lenses, compact construction, comparatively light weight, and legendary Leupold quality. My lead instructor's Air Arms PCP rifle has one, and its $400 price seems justifiable on a gun of such quality.

Nikon: The Prostaff Target EFR is a 3-9x40mm scope with an extreme-focus objective lens similar to the Leupold. It comes with a "precision reticle", which has fine duplex-type crosshairs. The scope is of average

Hawke Airmax 3-9 x 40 mm adjustable objective lens.

proportions and weight, making it another good all-around airgun scope choice. The adjustable objective permits very close-range use, and cost is under $200.

Others - Nikko Stirling, Leapers, BSA, Swift: My son has a Niko Stirling mounted to his Beeman/HW-97 spring rifle. It's a fairly large scope, but not to the point of excess. It's still hanging in there, too. I have only limited experience with the other brands, which are frequently mounted to airguns. A knowledgeable salesman at a major sporting retail store said he'd had good luck with BSA Airgun scopes on spring rifles.

Nikko Stirling 4-16 x 44 Platinum Scope with side-mounted parallax adjustment.

One thing to watch out for is a large scope on a barrel-cocking rifle. If it extends too far forward, you won't be able to cock the gun! You'll also need some type of scope stop to prevent recoil-induced movement. The heavier the scope, the more it'll want to creep. A lighter scope not only helps prevent this situation, but may also contribute to less hold sensitivity with spring guns. There's just less overall mass to move about.

MOUNTING SYSTEMS

Most airguns, whether spring or pre-charged models, have receivers with 11mm grooves. They'll often accept the same scope mounts sold for .22 rimfire rifles. Unfortunately, the reverse recoil of a springer will often cause a seemingly well-fitted set to creep rearward from inertia.

The RWS M-34 has a stop screw that protrudes from the rear of its factory-mounted scope base. Positioning a scope ring (or one-piece mount) to bear against the screw head will help prevent slippage. I've successfully used a pair of .22 rings on this rifle with a smaller scope. The Beeman R-9 sold by Pyramyd Air comes with a set of one-inch rings. A stud in

Airgun rings, securely mounted to the 11mm grooves of a Beeman R-9.

the bottom is designed to engage one of several corresponding holes that are centered between the receiver's grooves. The Sportsmatch rings are ideal, and Leapers or UTG sell similar ring sets. Lacking either of these features (or in addition to them), a scope stop can be purchased. It's a small block that firmly clamps to the rifle's scope base and serves as an arresting device. A bit of thread-locking compound can provide further anti-slip resistance.

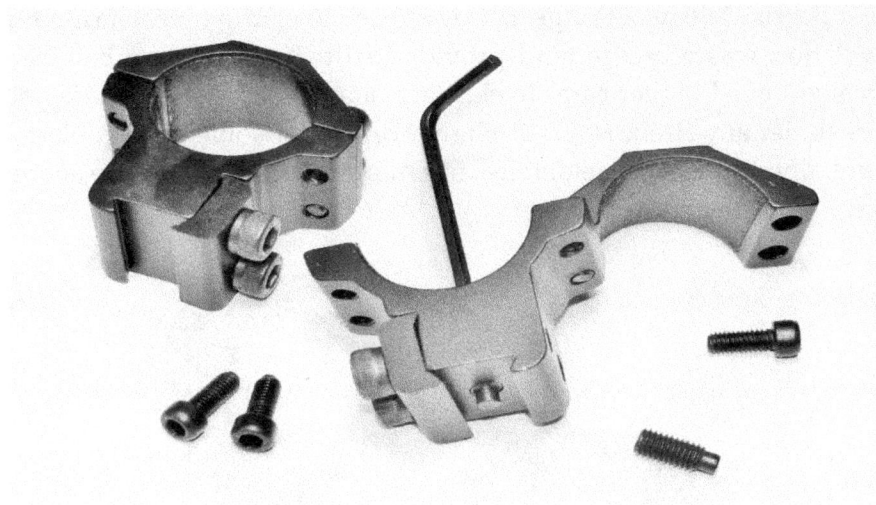

Tech Force scope rings, showing the recoil stop-screw, along with an included spare.

One-piece base and ring mounts are another often-seen design frequently sold with RWS scope packages. They typically employ a series of cap screws that firmly secure the base to the rifle. The ring spacing is usually fixed on these systems, which *could* cause mounting problems with some scopes. In fact, there are two different base lengths on RWS rifles, which can cause compatibility issues with some mounts. Also, the increased scope and base mass could also still creep rearward without some sort of mechanical stop. In some cases, the same bottom stud idea is incorporated. The latest idea is Diana's Bullseye Zero Recoil Mount, which has a built-in spring-loaded shock absorber feature. It even has built-in barrel droop compensation.

Diana's Bullseye Zero Recoil Mount is a solution to many airgun problems.

You can also buy adapter bases that attach to grooved receivers. The upper faces of the adapters are machined for Weaver or Picatinny scope rings, and the bottom surface clamps into the receiver. Tremendous mounting options can then be gained at the expense of extra height. BKL has an extensive line of mounting solutions, as do the others.

Pre-charged guns can be a whole lot simpler. I mounted a Burris 3-9 AO scope to my Air Arms PCP rifle, using a pair of Burris Deluxe .22 rings. It was as easy to clamp on each ring for optimum scope spacing. The installation was a breeze, and provided sufficient objective bell clearance above the barrel. A repeater might need higher rings to clear a magazine. Larger objective housings and lower rings may not work under any circumstances. Higher rings may solve that problem, at the expense of a proper gun mount. The Devil is in the details, and moderation helps ensure success.

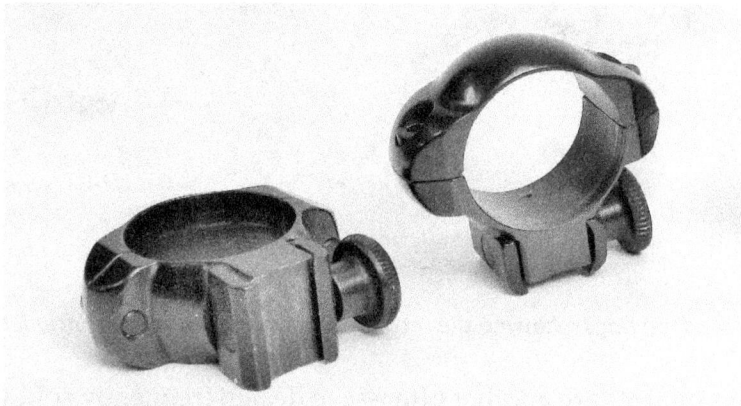

These tip-off scope rings are designed to fit the grooved receivers of most .22 rifles, but will work on some PCP rifles.

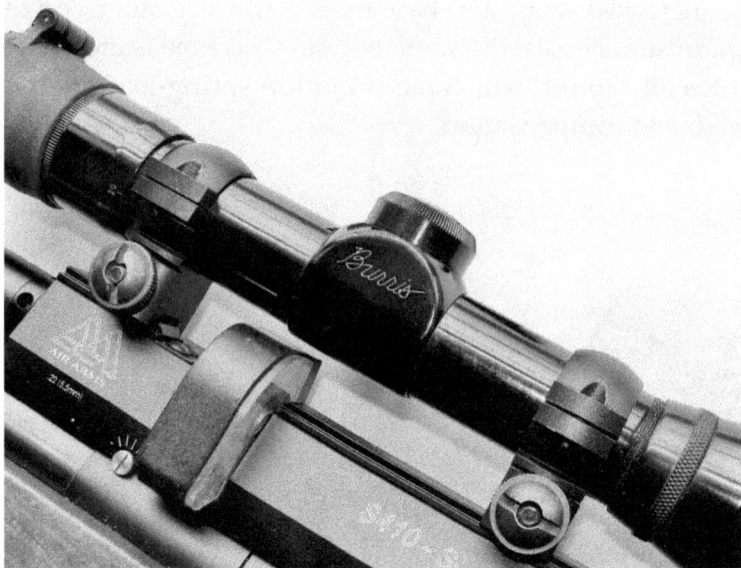

Adequate ring height will be necessary to clear protrusions like magazines. This inexpensive tip-off .22 ring set worked perfectly.

As for the actual scope mounting process, before putting everything together, it's wise to start with clean and dry surfaces. Mounting grooves can accumulate dirt and oil, which contribute to slippage. Oily rings will have less purchase on a scope tube. A clean fine brush and rag will take care of business with a bit of denatured alcohol. It's worth lightly assembling everything first, just to iron out ring and scope spacing issues. This is the time to ascertain the needed eye relief, as well as its leveling. It will need to be slid and rotated in the rings until everything seems right. The scope's reticle can be eyeballed or mechanically leveled, but those with ballistic aiming reticles should be as plumb as possible. It'll also need to stay put as the process continues.

After that, some sort of uniform tightening process is important. The ring halves should have similar gaps on each side. A tiny bit of clearance between the rings and turret and lens housings is worthwhile insurance against damage from slippage. An alternating tightening pattern will maintain uniform screw tensions. Most systems employ Allen wrenches, and the smaller end is best until the end, at which point a switch will serve for the final tightening. Too much, and you can dent a scope tube or strip out a screw. Too little, and slippage will result. If in doubt, seek a professional.

A great resource for bases, rings and mounting information is the Pyramyd Air website. Be sure to check out their "Airgun Academy".

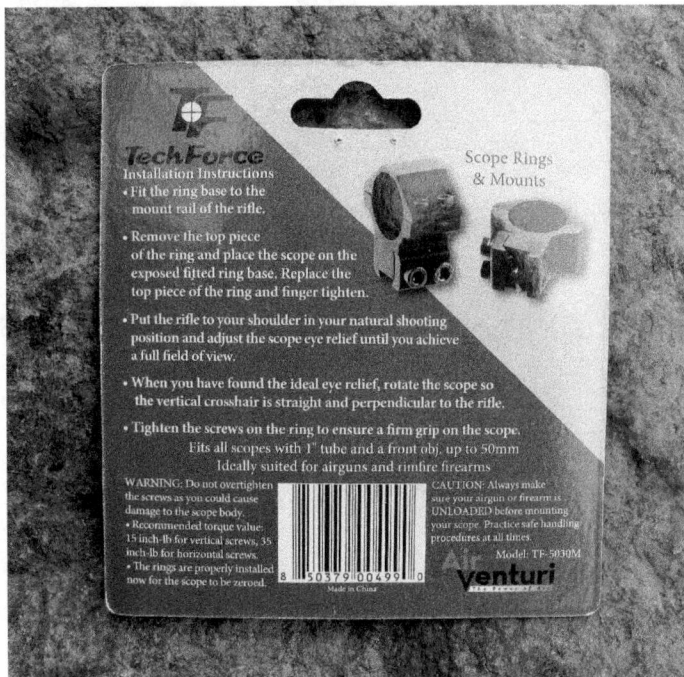

The directions on the packaging sum things up.

DOT SIGHTS

Most of these sights are electronic and non-magnifying. The shooter sees a red or green dot, which is superimposed on the target from an internal prism. Some designs also display circles, crosshairs, or even selectable options. A rheostat may permit the user to regulate the dot's intensity for varying light conditions. Confusion seems to exist between dot sights and lasers. Each is a totally different design, the laser projecting an external and concentrated beam of red or green light. A dot sight's aiming point is strictly internal and visible only within the sight body.

With dot sights, since no magnification is involved, field of view is huge and eye relief is a non-issue. In other words, they're fast to get on target. The dot's size is typically expressed in minutes-of-angle. A 6.5 MOA dot will cover roughly 6 ½ inches at 100 yards. At 300 yards, it will cover nearly 20 inches. This size is good for close-quarters shooting, but small targets will be hard to hit because they can disappear behind the dot. I don't like them for all-around use, but for close and fast shooting, they're just the ticket. A 2 MOA dot is my personal preference, providing a nice balance of speed and precision. However, it's not the right choice for tiny targets or those at long range. For those, you'll need a scope. An adjustable parallax feature isn't offered or needed.

An assortment of tube and tubeless dot-sights spanning the full gamut of pricing from under a C-note to several hundred dollars.

Very small, tubeless sights are becoming more popular. They resemble miniature, pre-flat screen TV sets, and are extremely compact. Most, but not all, require dismounting during battery changes. Afterwards, you'll need a new zero. I have three generations of Burris Fast-Fire sights, and the latest FF-III solves this problem. The battery compartment has been relocated topside, permitting easy changes. Still, at over $200, it may not appeal to everyone.

Electronics can fail, and the lower-priced models will more than likely quit at some point. I'm not sure how long *any* of these electronic devices would survive on a spring or gas piston gun. The smallest units have little mass, but their circuitry might be damaged through repeat vibrations. In our experience, most people don't shoot a dot more accurately than a receiver sight anyway, although the former is faster. A safer springer bet would probably be a peep sight in conjunction with a fiber-optic front sight – assuming the heights will properly match up.

One thing to keep in mind is that many dot sights are designed for Weaver or Picatinny-type bases. However, most airguns are machined with grooved receivers that accept .22 rimfire tip-off scope rings. The systems are completely different, which could pose a real mounting problem. Conversion bases are sold, assuming you can locate one that fits your particular airgun's receiver. In some cases, you may be able to get creative. Using the B-Square (or similar Hawke) grooved receiver/Weaver base adapters, you could probably mount a dot sight to the Intermount base on a Benjamin pump-up rifle. Without any eye relief limitations, it could be located well forward for unimpeded pumping.

The PCP rifles are so accurate and powerful that they really deserve a scope, but the Benjamin Marauder pistol seems like a great candidate for a dot sight. The smallest types would maintain its sleek lines whether configured as a pistol or a carbine. The miniature units only weigh a few ounces, and occupy little mounting space. High-end miniaturized dots are sold by Trijicon, Leupold, and others. You'll pay more for the sights than you will for an M-pistol. Since battlefield conditions won't be a concern, we can do a bit better, pricewise.

One thing to keep in mind is that these miniature sights have Weaver/Picatinny-type bases. But by using a single dovetail adapter, you should be able to mount one to a Marauder Pistol.

Burris Fast-Fire: This small sight has gone through three evolutions, and I have them all. The FF-III is the most user-friendly, but it's also the most expensive at around $250. Like the somewhat simpler and less expensive FF-II, its main attribute is very compact size. On a pistol, the cheaper $200 version will work just fine. Unlike the FF-III, it'll need to be dismounted for battery changes. Then again, pellets are cheap, so a re-zero is no big deal. The FF-II has a 4 MOA red dot and friction adjustments. The FF-III has a slightly finer 3 MOA dot with clickstops and an intensity adjustment. They all run on a CR-2032

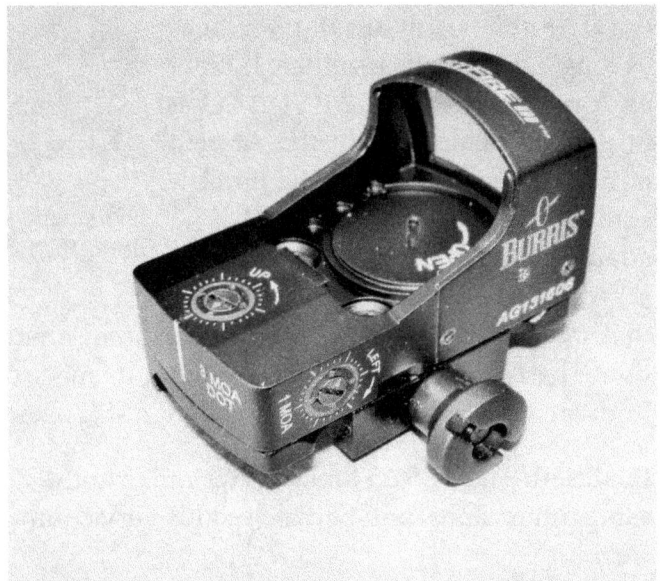

The ultra-compact Burris Fast-Fire III permits battery replacement without loss of zero.

coin-type battery. The original FF-I isn't waterproof, but the others are.

Redfield Accelerator: Here's another small sight, similar to the Burris. It has a larger 6 MOA dot with L, M, H, & Auto intensity settings. It also runs off a CR-2032 battery that can be replaced without dismounting the unit. An adapter is available that permits mounting of the Redfield to the bases of some other manufacturers' units. Grooved or 11 mm dovetails may still be problematic, but a conversion base can solve this problem. Cost is $200, with a "no excuses" warranty.

Bushnell First Strike: This sight presents a viable alternative, for a few small sacrifices in features. The 5 MOA dot runs on an auto-adjust sensor. Unlike the Burris and Redfield units, it has no on/off switch. Instead, replacement of its plastic cover shuts the Bushnell off. Replacement of the CR-2032 battery requires disassembly and re-zeroing, but like the others, this sight is waterproof. It also comes with an AR-15 riser block. The warranty is one year, but the price is only $110.

Other small dot sights: There are a bunch of them. None will need to withstand any recoil forces on a PCP pistol or pump-up rifle. Just surf the net and look for product reviews.

Konus Atomic: Unlike the miniature TV-types, this one has a tubular body. However, it's not a whole lot bigger. I have one mounted to a combination gun, and so far the Atomic has withstood its not-quite-nuclear 12 gauge recoil. A side-mounted dial permits five different intensity settings, in choices of red or green dot colors. An "off" setting powers down the 4 MOA dot. The unit is only around 2 ½ inches long, and weighs less than 4 ounces. It runs off a CR-2032 battery. One neat item included with the Atomic is a B-Square adapter. My Finnish combo-gun has an 11mm rail. The adapter slips right on and provides a Weaver-type mounting conversion

This Konus Atomic has so far survived the recoil of a 12 gauge/.223 combination gun. A pair of B-Square dovetail/Weaver adapter bases was used. The forward one serves merely as a spacer. The one under the sight was included in its packaging.

that matches this sight. It should work the same way on a Marauder Pistol for hassle-free installation. The Atomic should also fit behind its magazine, at the rear of the receiver. I bought mine from Midway USA several years ago, and it's still listed for around $100 with a limited lifetime warranty.

Bushnell: The TRS-25 looks very similar to the Atomic, but has a 3 MOA red dot. It also shares the same dimensions (and battery), so it's very compact. Cost is around $100, and it comes with a 2-year warranty.

Bushnell, among others, also sells a line of larger tube-type dot sights that mount in standard scope rings. By selecting the right set, you could mount one directly to the receiver of a Marauder or other 11 mm/grooved set of dovetails.

Since these sights all run on batteries, it's worth having a few spares on hand. They'll all die at some point, and one common cause is operator error. Although their lowest settings are useful in dim light, a faint dot is easy to miss after sunup. I've put more than one away when it was still turned on.

CHAPTER 9

AIRGUN SAFETY

This topic is covered more thoroughly in *Survival Guns: A Beginner's Guide*. Condensed versions were also carried forward in the subsequent editions, including the recent *Rimfire Rifles: A Buyer's and Shooter's Guide*. That recap is presented here. In essence, by following a few basic rules at all times, we should be able to safely handle and fire any type of gun without endangering ourselves or others.

Folks sometimes adopt a dismissive attitude about airgun safety, perhaps largely due to their perceived power. However, airgun projectiles claim lives every year. Like a firearm, an airgun is no toy! A proper backstop is essential. The lowliest rimfire loads can penetrate a human skull or chest cavity, as can airgun projectiles. Don't attempt to fire a shot until the five "Universal Firearms Safety Rules" can be recited by heart.

THE UNIVERSAL SAFETY RULES

#1: Treat all firearms as if loaded! We don't care if the safety is on or not, or whether the gun is unloaded. It doesn't matter if the action is open or closed. It's *ALWAYS* loaded, and should never sweep any part of you, or anyone else!

#2: Don't allow the muzzle to sweep something you're unwilling to destroy! This rule *always* applies, whether during handling or in storage. Further caution will be necessary when using a sling. If carried muzzle-up, it's easy to sweep others while bending forward, and a careless rearward dismount can produce the same effect. Be aware of your muzzle at all times!

#3: Keep your finger off the trigger until ready to fire! Find an index point on the gun. Typically, the trigger finger will be extended forward, parallel with the bottom of the receiver. You can disengage a safety while committing to fire, but the trigger is off limits until the gun is fully mounted. You can also bet that most "accidental" shootings are the result of a failure to follow this rule, as well as the others. The safety is never a substitute for sloppy muzzle discipline. YOU are the safety!

#4: Be sure of your target, and what is beyond it! Airgun projectiles will routinely carry several hundred yards. The latest big bore types may travel a half-mile. If you shoot it, you own it! An adequate backstop is essential. We need to exercise situational awareness at all times and manage our muzzles accordingly.

#5: Check any type of gun upon handling it. Don't just assume a gun is unloaded. However, airgun designs pose increased challenges, since there is generally no eye-catching cartridge. We'll deal with the unique concerns in a moment. Recently, I was in a well-known gun shop. Next to the cash register, a small piece of wood was missing from the counter. As it turned out, a customer had dropped off a pre-charged airgun. No one fully understood its basic operation. Miraculously, although all five safety rules were violated, the only casualty was the omnipresent reminder that appeared within close proximity to a sales person. Bottom line: if you don't know how a gun works, leave it alone!

AIRGUN SAFETY AND DESIGN LIMITATIONS

Proper gun etiquette dictates that a firearm should be passed to someone unloaded and on "safe". Its action should be open, and the recipient should immediately check it as well. However, airguns sometimes pose a problem due to their designs.

Chamber checks: In this case, we're referring to the breech of an airgun. The load status of a barrel-cocking airgun is relatively easy to verify. You can crack it open far enough to inspect the breech and safely look through the entire bore. If the barrel easily pivots downward, the gun is already cocked.

Most other types won't provide as simple a method for a thorough visual inspection. Under and side lever springers can usually be manipulated to view their loading ports and a small portion of their barrel breeches. Any normally loaded pellet *should* be evident.

The probe on a pump-up or PCP gun will seat a pellet past its transfer port, well inside the barrel. You *could* look through the muzzle end, but natural selection may prevail. I'd rather open the action and carefully run a rod through the muzzle until it emerges at the breech. A length of 3/16" dowel will suffice, and it can also be used to unload a pellet. Truthfully, I'd prefer to shoot the gun in a safe direction. That won't hurt a pneumatic system, but it could damage an unloaded springer. The insertion of a felt cleaning pellet is good insurance for types with limited breech access.

A barrel-cocking safety check is easy. Note the rifling, seal, and spring-loaded locking stud.

The breech of an under-lever HW 97-K, showing a bit of the bore exposed. A rod-check is a safer bet.

Before passing my PCP rifle to anyone else, I first explain its limitations. I then place the gun on "safe" and pull the bolt back just far enough to ensure that it isn't cocked. Why not just fully open the bolt? For starters, at that point, the gun will be cocked. Also, if the trigger was accidentally pulled, the lug that engages the internal valve striker might be sheared off. So instead, I explain the process, and the gun's muzzle is carefully managed at all times. When returning from the field, I'll discharge it prior to entering a vehicle or dwelling. At that point, the gun will be uncocked and its bore will be clear *if* adequate pressure remains. The report should be a good indication, but I still like to point the muzzle near a few blades of grass above a soft surface.

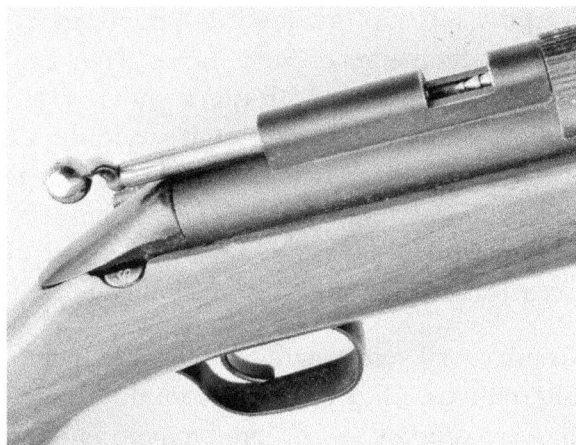

The brass jag on a cleaning rod indicates a clear bore. Note the safety in its "on" position.

BACKSTOPS AND TARGETS

Some airgun pellets have fairly short maximum carrying ranges of a quarter mile or less. Others will travel quite a bit further, but all are potentially dangerous within their full carrying distances. An adequate backstop is essential, and airguns present some unique concerns.

Backstops: BBs are made from steel that won't compress or splatter upon impact with hard surfaces. Instead, they'll ricochet with considerable force. A large cardboard box stuffed full of rags is a safer bet for stopping them. The same is true with lower-velocity pellets, which have a tendency to bounce off some materials like wood, leaving just a shallow depression. Medium-velocity pellets will often stick in, exposing their skirts. Higher-velocity pellets will penetrate quite a distance and may even pass through strapping or plywood. Everything will seem fine until one hits a knot, another buried pellet, or the end grain of a stump. Suddenly, you'll face a nasty ricochet.

I have an old steel bullet trap in the basement, designed to safely capture .22 rimfire bullets. It'll safely contain any lead pellets, but their impact is fairly loud. Lead residue is another concern, especially around children. More often than not I shoot pellets outdoors on my small-bore range, which has an earthen berm.

This ancient Detroit bullet trap is rated for .22 Long Rifle rounds. It has safely captured thousands of pellets. Something to consider is lead dust.

Targets: Some of my favorite targets are 3/16" thick steel disks in diameters of 3 to 6 inches. They ring when hit, and can be touched up with quick shots of spray paint. Lead pellets shatter upon impact at straight-on angles, leaving a visible mark and just a thin remaining lead wafer. Shooting distances range from no closer than 15 yards out to 50 yards or further. An 8-inch plate hangs at 100 yards for the occasional long-range airgun challenge.

Commercial soft, reactive targets are increasingly popular alternatives. They're made from durable self-healing synthetic materials. Many are shaped as squirrels, birds, or diamonds, which spin on a bracket when hit. Mine carry warnings about use of airgun projectiles. While .22 LR bullets will pass through them, pellets can embed or bounce off with the same hazards as wood.

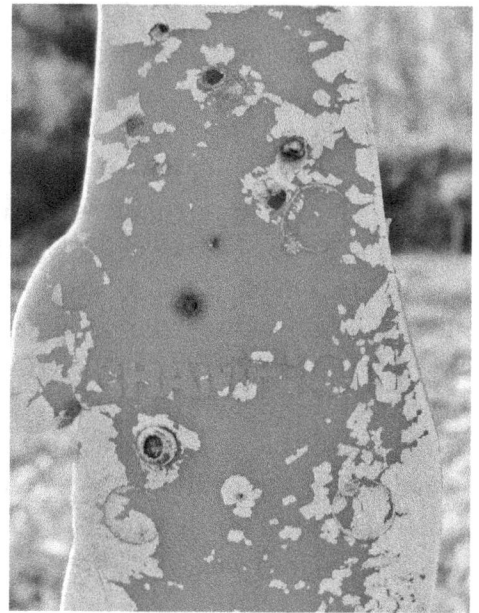

Life is full of surprises, and common sense can prevent many that are unpleasant. From experience, I can state that golf balls and airguns definitely don't mix. Plan on fast-traveling ricochet! Shooting a pellet at a live primer can produce another memorable event (assuming one's frontal lobe remains intact). Sheet metal can be exciting, too.

Look closely and you'll see .22 pellets imbedded in the surface of this synthetic target from 50 yards. Others shot at lower velocities bounced off.

Before firing a shot, track down a good set of shooting glasses and make sure everyone else is properly equipped.

SYSTEM CAUTIONS

Most of the airgun systems have unique pitfalls that can easily be avoided with proper knowledge and common sense.

Springers: During the cocking and loading process, it's wise to maintain a secure grasp at all times. If a cocking arm or barrel is accidentally released, it will snap forward with great force. A serious injury could result, as well as a bent barrel. Disassembly of these guns requires a special fixture that contains the mainspring and its retaining cap as tension is gradually relieved. This tool resembles an extra-long threaded clamp. Without it, both parts will exit the rear of

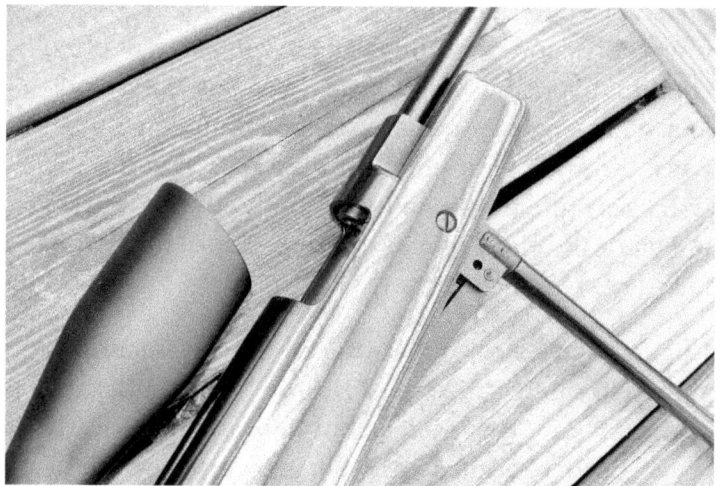

Maintain control of a spring-gun's cocking system. Think about where your fingers will be during loading!

the compression tube with considerable force. In other words, don't take one apart! The correct lubricants are also necessary to prevent ignition during the brief but intense pressure cycle within the gun.

CO2 guns: Carbon dioxide is a temperature-sensitive gas, and heat can elevate pressure to unsafe levels. A bottle inside a trunk or hot car could rupture, so these systems need to be located away from strong sunlight or heat. Caution is also necessary during pressurization and handling. Make sure the gun is unloaded, and wear safety glasses.

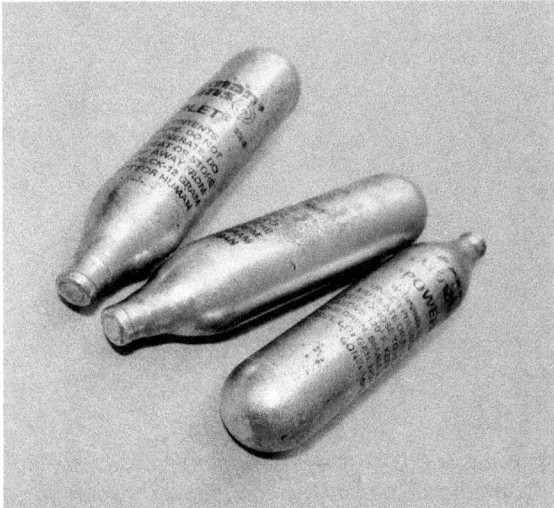

It's easy to forget that CO-2 cartridges are under pressure. Handle and store them accordingly.

Pre-charged pneumatics: High-pressure air isn't as temperature-sensitive as CO2, but you can still get in trouble with a hot scuba tank. If it bursts or is dropped, the 3000 psi charge can turn it into a bomb or rocket. This pressure also demands full attention during connection to the gun or when bleeding off the hose. Safety glasses are strongly advised! It's easy to forget that a fully charged PCP gun has a pressurized reservoir. It should undergo periodic inspections, especially if charged

from a hand pump. This is a requirement with scuba tanks. Overcharging a gun won't increase its velocity, and could result in a rupture with flying parts. Substituting another source of pressure (like oxygen) is *extremely* dangerous. So is use of the wrong lubricants, which could detonate under pressure. The fill attachments for most PCP guns connect near the muzzle, so exercise caution and make sure the gun is unloaded and on "safe" before proceeding.

Respect the muzzle when filling a pre-charged airgun. Think about your fittings, too. This stainless-steel female connection is HPA-rated. The brass paintball types can rupture. Safety glasses are worthwhile around this technology.

OTHER CAUTIONS

Airguns occupy a unique field when compared to firearms. There are legions of veterans who can fully disassemble an M16 while blindfolded. When reassembled, it will likely be spotlessly clean and well oiled. Transferring these skills to air-powered systems can cause well-intentioned problems. Even though real men don't read directions, it's sometimes a good idea.

Lubricants: As noted above, you can get in a heap of trouble with the wrong types. Best case: the seals on a pump-up gun become damaged to the point where they won't hold air. Worse case: an explosion occurs inside a pre-charged pneumatic that is already pressurized to 2900 psi. The Airgun Maintenance chapter addresses these worries.

Trigger adjustments: Many airguns have adjustable triggers. Pull weights can vary considerably, and are often commensurate with costs. Anything adjustable invites "adjusting" which, in the case of a trigger, isn't always prudent. True, a stiff or gritty trigger pull is a real impediment to accuracy. On the other hand, one that is very light can invite an inadvertent discharge. I really don't like pull much below three pounds for any type of gun carried afield. This use is much different from the controlled conditions common to target shooting disciplines. Since the majority of firearms intended for real world use are furnished with trigger pulls of three pounds or more, mastery of a similar airgun weight is beneficial. An improperly adjusted trigger poses further concerns related to spring guns and flying cocking systems. For those that feel compelled to tweak a trigger, an owner's manual is highly recommended!

This easily adjustable R-9 trigger invites tweaking. Don't get carried away, and follow the manufacturer's instructions!

More pressure issues: The concerns about uncontrolled spring-powered parts are real. A barrel that slips from a shooter's grasp, or a flying end cap, is a fast-moving object propelled by spring pressure. The pre-charged guns can be even more energetic when under pressure. It's best to have them serviced by a professional. I did fix a slow leak in a PCP rifle after consulting with a respected airgun dealer. It was actually a simple process, *after* depressurizing the unloaded gun! An unusual hazard is associated with CO_2 guns; sudden depressurization could actually cause frostbite to any nearby fingers. One last point: even without a pellet, the blast of pressure emitted from the muzzle of any airgun could be very harmful at close range. Practice safe gun handling at all times!

Stuck pellets: Decreasing pressure can cause a pellet to lodge in a barrel. A PCP gun near the bottom end of its air charge can create this hazard, and the same is true of CO_2 designs. Insufficiently charged pump-up types may also lack adequate pressure to expel a projectile. Again, always follow the safety rules. *Assume the gun is loaded, and handle it accordingly!* Also, don't attempt to reuse fired pellets. It's another great way to wind up with one lodged in a barrel. It may stick hard enough to cause damage during removal.

Lead: The discharge of conventional airgun pellets involves some exposure to lead. It's not as big a problem as firearms ammunition, but it's still a concern. In fact, at times, it may be a greater issue. An indoor airgun range is entirely doable, but those involving steel bullet traps can generate lead dust during pellet impacts. We all know that lead paint is a significant health hazard, something shooters should be mindful of as well.

Safety gear: Before firing a shot, track down a good set of shooting glasses. Wear them anytime airguns are discharged in your proximity, and make sure everyone else is properly equipped. Airgun projectiles can ricochet off trees, knock-down targets, or a variety of other things. Why risk losing an eye?

Mindset: Last week, I attended a meeting about some upcoming sniper training. We brought in a highly experienced subject matter expert to help design the program. Later on, the subject of our British PCP air rifles came up. We got a blank look, followed by "oh yeah, you mean BB guns!" Well, no, we didn't mean that at all. And that's the problem; many knowledgeable firearms people fail to take these systems seriously. Again, they're not toys! Treat them with the upmost respect! It goes without saying that alcohol and drugs don't mix. Neither do unsupervised children or others who raise similar concerns. Unattended guns are a huge problem, requiring responsible storage. Firearms safety and storage is covered in depth within *Survival Guns: A Beginner's Guide*.

CHAPTER 10

ZERO, ACCURACY AND RANGE

With a suitable and properly equipped airgun on hand, it's time to do some shooting. Our first step should involve capturing some shots on a target. Next, we can make sight adjustments until they strike the same approximate aiming spot at a constant distance. At that point, we'll be "sighted in". From there, we can perform some valid accuracy testing by shooting various pellet types.

Higher gun prices normally ensure better quality that leads to better accuracy, but consistent pellets play a key part. In fact, without them, any serious testing efforts are really just a waste of time. The cheaper pellets are less uniform, meaning they *can't* achieve great accuracy. It's also entirely possible that a quality pellet just *won't* shoot well in one particular gun. There are a number of reasons, ranging from dimensional tolerances to barrel harmonics. In other words, shooters should try several *good* brands.

A PELLET SAMPLER KIT

For just a bit more money than basic bargain pellets, you can purchase consistent types. Some of the manufacturers offer their pellet tins in different quantities. Instead of blindly ordering large containers, you could try a few smaller tins, or even buy a sampler package. You'll probably need to mail-order them so, once again, and Airguns of Arizona, Pyramyd Air, or Pomona Airguns are great sources with plenty of choices.

Good bets: Some of the brands I'd try include Beeman, Crosman Premier, H&N, JSB, and RWS. Unless I had a very powerful rifle, I'd stick with mid-weight domed types. My short list would include JSB Exacts and Crosman Premiers. Spring rifle

Those starting from scratch could try JSB pellets or the Crosman match-grade Premiers sold in a 625-count brown box.

shooters should choose relatively tight-fitting pellets to maintain piston-cushioning back pressure. A snug breech fit will also help prevent pellets from falling out of barrel-cocking guns during the loading process. Some shooters seat them with a small tool or ballpoint pen tip.

SIGHTING IN

A good steady rest is necessary, along with calm conditions. We'll address this more thoroughly in a moment. For now, the idea is to make the adjustments necessary to place a series of pellets on or near your intended spot. A group that forms near the center of a paper target will suffice. We can fine-tune everything later.

Think about the velocity of your gun and choose an appropriate distance. For average spring guns, the distance might be 30 yards; for PCP types, it could be 40 paces. An iron-sighted pump-up rifle might do better if zeroed at 20 to 25 yards. It's really up to the shooter, and these distances are just guidelines.

Because of their designs, most airguns can't be bore sighted, so you may want to start at a distance of 10 yards. With spring guns, it might be worthwhile to begin even closer. The odds will be better of capturing a pellet somewhere on the target. Remember the droop problem common with some air rifles? It's possible that some gun and scope mounting systems may be grossly out of alignment. There's nothing more frustrating than firing a shot that completely misses the target.

Instead of randomly cranking in scope adjustments, we can apply some mechanical logic. Consider the height of the crosshairs above the bore. At *very* close range, when a pellet is shot, the resulting impact should show the same approximate divergence. Let's say, after measurement, a scope height of around 1 ½ inches is determined. If you back out just a few steps from the target and shoot, a hole noticeably lower than that might indicate droop. You'll want to shoot a few pellets, just to make sure. Assuming both measurements coincide, the next stop might be 10 yards. Somewhere within these distances, you should be able to detect any alignment problems related to elevation or windage. These steps can save a lot of aggravation, as well as some ammo.

After that, you can increase the distance and establish a good baseline zero. This is also a good time to work on all of the shooting basics, with extra attention paid to follow-through. Remember: pellets will spend a bit more time inside your barrel than high-velocity bullets. A PCP rifle will be recoilless so, with concentration at further distances, you may be able to see your pellets arc through the scope and punch holes in your target. If so, your follow-through is excellent. Especially at longer ranges, the looping trajectory is educational.

Springers are a whole different animal, requiring special methods. Essentially, you'll be applying just the minimum effort to ensure relative stability. With practice, you should be able to develop a successful technique. In general, the more potent the gun, the fussier it will be. Once in a while you may hit a springer that can be placed directly on a rest, but it's not common.

This bench rest set-up will work with firearms or pre-charged rifles, but a springer will probably need a softer interface. The bags can be used as hand supports.

Iron sight shooters will need to move their rear sight in the direction they want a pellet to go. Shoot at least three shots (five are even better) before touching anything. If the group develops below the target, the rear sight will need to be raised. Shots striking left means the rear sight should move right. Often, the sights have small index scales to help keep track of adjustments. Some guns get their elevation adjustments off the front sight. In that case, move it in reverse. Either way, we're trying to get the sighting plane and barrel to coincide at a precise spot downrange. Actually, the bore will need a bit of extra elevation relative to the line of sight. This discrepancy will compensate for the arc of the pellet.

Shooters using optical sights can follow the adjustment indicators on their turrets. More often than not, there is an arrow by a "U" or "Right" to indicate desired changes. A low hit would require movements upwards. As often as not, graduations on each dial will provide some idea how much. Let's say your group forms four inches low at 25 yards. Removing the elevation cap (on top) we see a scale indicating each click equals either a ¼ MOA, or ¼ inch at 100 yards. Well, at 25 yards, the angular discrepancies would be less. Each click would only be one fourth those values, or roughly 1/16 inch. We'd need to carefully count clicks while moving the elevation dial upwards 64 clicks. Some turrets have a moveable indicator that can be rotated in alignment with a witness mark after sighting in. It's worth using, and provides a frame of reference during subsequent tuning.

Typical scope turret: each click equals ¼" of reticle movement at 100 yards. or approximately ¼ MOA at any range.

With some barrel-cocking springer and scope combinations, sufficient elevation adjustments may not be possible. If so, the problem may be barrel droop. In that case, a drooper mount could fix the problem. Don't force scope adjustments. Ideally, we should be somewhere towards the center of the adjustment ranges.

A baseline zero: You may want to begin with a tin of Crosman 14.3 grain Premiers. Ultimately, they might not produce the best accuracy, but performance will likely be adequate to help refine your skills. Don't forget that spring rifles sometimes need a break-in period before meaningful accuracy testing is possible. Also, different pellets will probably shoot to different spots.

If groups seem unusually large or random, check for loose stock screws and scope mounts. They're a common problem with the more powerful spring guns. With cheap scopes it's not unusual to see a sudden shift in pellet impacts. The reticle is housed within a separate internal tube, located in proximity to the turrets. Spring pressure will hopefully exert sufficient force to keep it bearing against the turret contacts. That doesn't always happen with inexpensive scopes like those in gun packages. Some jump around during the harsh recoil of spring rifles, often without warning. That's *really* irritating! Try returning it; or swap it out for something better.

Once you have a workable zero, further accuracy research can prove valuable. You might stumble on to a winning gun and pellet combination right out of the gate. If so, it's time to stock up and have some fun. But, I wouldn't jump the gun. You might receive a rude awakening later on.

TESTING PHASES

Sometimes even a mediocre rifle can shine with the right load. Hit the winning combination and a decently accurate gun could become a real ringer. Because we're talking about airguns some readers may have an opportunity to experiment right on their premises. If so, good! The extra experience gained here may prove useful during centerfire trials.

The setup: Meaningful accuracy assessment requires elimination of the variables. Atmospherics are one, with wind playing a major factor. Temperature and light are other factors. Another issue is the human equation. We'll need a way to properly support our rifle with the minimum physical effects. Different techniques will be necessary, depending on whether or not a spring rifle is involved. Remember, they're often hold-sensitive, so firm rests are generally out. Stability isn't, though.

A permanent shooting bench is always preferred. Everything is locked in due to a solid shooting position.

A good starting point is a solid shooting bench. A flimsy card table can help get you sighted in, but it won't cut the mustard for accuracy assessments. A car hood or other makeshift foundation won't, either. One beauty of an airgun is that you can shoot it in lots of places, including some backyards. But in this case, we need a good shooting bench like those commonly found at ranges. It's probably worth a trip, if you can nail calm conditions. There are commercial portable units too, like Caldwell's Stable Table. With a solid foundation established, we'll need some type of consistent rifle support. I'm partial to the heavy metal rests with three wide legs and an adjustable cradle designed for a sandbag. Again, Caldwell comes through with "The Rock", which comes with two necessary sandbags. The second one is positioned between the rifle's stock and the bench surface. Some time for careful setup is needed to ensure comfort. The rifle should line up naturally and without contortions. A proper seat is part of the process.

The Caldwell Stable Table breaks down into several pieces for transportation. It will easily fit in the trunk of car.

Here's "The Rock", with connotations of stability, which it does indeed provide. Inexpensive furniture glides help protect the bench top from its pointed feet.

If everything is right, the rifle's forend will be nestled in the front bag, atop the rest. The rear bag will support the bottom rear of the stock. This arrangement will work with guns other than springers. Some sort of soft contact is needed with guns of this type to minimize vibrations. A few layers of thick towel laid over the front rest can help support the back of your support hand, which can be gingerly located for minimum interference. The stock may be free-floating or just lightly contacting something soft. Pillows aren't a bad substitute if you can work out the right heights. Some of the newer, large parallel bag supports may be even

Cabelas sells a folding "Herters" bench that sets up in seconds, much like an ironing board. It'll stand up in a closet or slip in the bed of a pickup truck, but it's too long for most car trunks.

better. Whatever is chosen, you may wind up exchanging total stability for a compromise system that minimizes transferred vibration. It'll take real concentration and strict adherence to marksmanship principles for meaningful results.

Accuracy: Final accuracy determinations should be based on a number of consistent groups shot during optimum conditions, at the same distances, and on the same type of targets. A fairly universal testing range for rimfire .22 rifles is 50 yards. That's a bit of a stretch for most airguns, but I still wouldn't rule it out as part of a two-phase protocol. To a large extent, it depends on the type of airgun and its sighting system. With an iron-sighted pump-up rifle, 25 yards will work. That range can also serve as Phase #1 with other guns. But with high performance scoped air rifles, I'd definitely want to shoot a Phase #2 series of groups at 40 or even 50 yards. These distances may be towards the outer practical limits of some guns, but any inconsistencies will be more clearly evident.

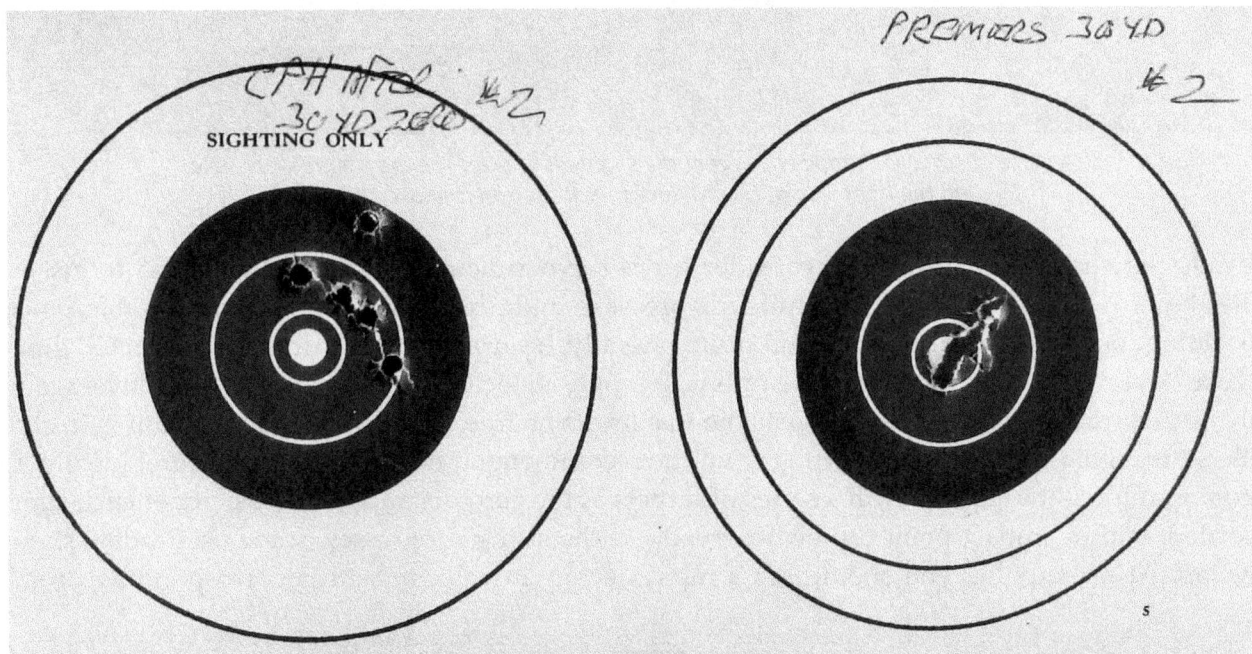

It pays to experiment. This test involved two types of Crosman .22 pellets: Premier Hollow-points (L), and the more expensive brown-box Premiers. Each group consists of 5 shots, fired from a Beeman R-9 at 30 yards.

Disappointments can often be cured through a simple pellet change. For example, wadcutters, which are the predominant match pellet choice, can do some wild stuff at longer ranges. Other types may just not be preferred by certain barrels. The proof is in some careful shooting. In fact, it may even take a few shots before groups settle down after switching pellets. It's best not to jump to conclusions based on just one or two groups. The biggest thing is consistency throughout the testing process. Still air is essential. When I can find it, I prefer to run at least two test series on different days in similar light and temperatures. Each series will consist of five 5-shot groups. Ten consistent targets can increase the odds of repeatable accuracy. Only then will I consider a bulk order. It's worth saving your targets or recording digital images for future reference. You never know when a winner might be out of stock or even discontinued. In that case, it's worth having a fallback choice.

A piece of surveyor's tape will reveal the slightest breeze. The crosshairs were held on the right side of the 40-yard metal squirrel to make this hit.

Pre-charged shooters may want to consider further experimentation before locking in to just one pellet type. Additional variables include air pressure and, for those rifles with adjustable power, the setting. Both will affect velocity and quite possibly, accuracy. It's not unusual for a PCP gun to have a "sweet spot" within its useable pressure range. Velocities can deviate from the average not only as pressure decreases, but also near the maximum charge. The best way to find out is to shoot pellets through a chronograph, starting from the recommended maximum air pressure. Ideally, the chronograph will be aligned with a series of targets at the zero distance. The velocity of each shot is recorded, and its impact point can be observed. As the string progresses, some useful data should develop. At some point, you should see a rapid decline in velocity with a corresponding drop in

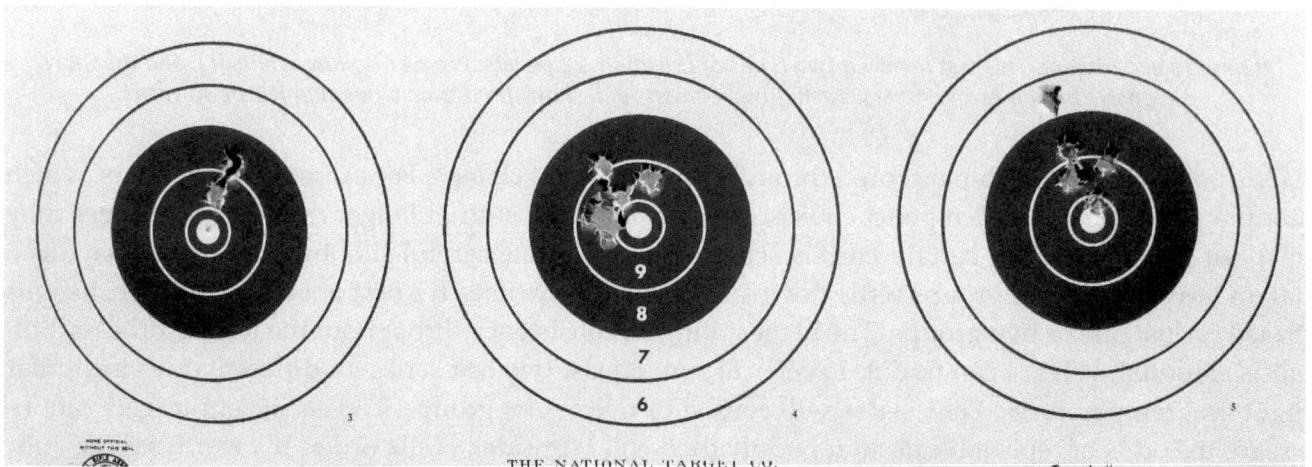

These 5-shot groups were shot from 30 yards in (L-R) still air and an increasing, quartering breeze. It doesn't take much wind to affect accuracy. The pellets were 15.9 grain JSBs launched at 900 fps.

pellet impacts. Some shooters use a computer to graph their shot strings and identify an optimum pressure range. But even without a chronograph, the targets alone will provide useful information. Of course, power setting adjustments change everything, including, quite possibly, accuracy results. Somewhere within the endless combinations lies a semblance of compromise. With that sorted out, it's time to think about another shooting escapade...

Establishing your final zero: One project worth trying involves shooting 5-shot groups in 10-yard increments, right out to 50 yards (or more). The results should reveal two things: your practical accuracy limit and your maximum practical range. Using this information, you can think about an optimum zero range. It will probably fall at a closer distance, somewhere in the midpoint of your pellet's arc. This strategy should help minimize elevation compensations related to trajectory.

For me, 15.9 grain domed .22 pellets with a 900 fps muzzle velocity work great when zeroed at 40 yards. I know this thanks to 10-yard incremental testing. Forty yards is my "default zero", and once established, the scope turrets are set to "0" on their indicators. In this case, the rifle is an Air Arms PCP Model 400 with adjustable power. Its rheostat setting is recorded, so if any changes happen, I can always find my way home.

If you're motivated, this trigger time is worthwhile. It may be trial and error, but sooner or later you'll come up with a practical zero distance. More shooting at other distances will allow you to plot your exact trajectory. This shooting will provide the necessary information for precise aiming compensations and reliable hits. You'll definitely want still air!

I recently laid out a 50-yard airgun range in order to gather some useful velocity and zero data. Targets were positioned in ten-yard increments, using a laser rangefinder. The test involved three different .22 air rifles set at 700, 800, and 900 fps. Based on previous experience, I used the zero distances shown in the chart below. Muzzle velocities were recorded during this test, and are an average of five shots. Interestingly, although the temperature was close to freezing that day, velocities were on par with much warmer results.

Slower pellets of the same weight have steeper trajectories, so for this test, each increase of 100 fps translated to a zero increase of five additional yards. Sure, I could've used one standard zero like 40 yards, but the mid-range crosshair deviations would've been much greater with 700 fps pellets. Instead, I matched sight-in distances to velocity categories, so hold-off allowances could be minimized.

AIR RIFLE VELOCITY & TRAJECTORY GUIDE: Deviation from point of aim in inches, using indicated zeros									
Test: 3/25/2015		Temperature: 35 F		Wind: Calm					
Air Rifle	Pellet	Grain	M.V.	Zero	10 Yd	20 Yd	30 Yd	40 Yd	50 Yd
Beeman R-9 Springer	.22 JSB	14.3	690 fps	30 Yd	- ¼"	+ ¼"	- 0 -	- 1 ¼"	- 4 ¼"
Air Arms 410-S PCP	.22 JSB	14.3	815 fps	35 Yd	- ¼"	+ ¼"	+ ¾"	- 3/4"	- 2"
Air Arms 400 ERB PCP	.22 JSB	15.9	918 fps	40 Yd	- ¼"	+4/10"	+ ½"	- 0 -	- 1"
Center of scopes approximately 1 ½" above center of bore									

As a further advantage, lighter 14.3 grain pellets were used in the less powerful guns to help boost their velocities and flatten trajectories. It's just easier to hit small targets when major aiming compensations are off the table. The maximum effective range may need to be shortened up a bit, but for me it's a worthwhile tradeoff.

On the other hand, the higher velocity of the AA 400 permits use of heavier pellets for a bit more downrange thump, without compromising effective range. At 900 fps, the gun is obviously still useful right out to 50 yards!

Scope height plays a role in these factors, with higher mounts causing greater divergence from the zero distance. One reason I like smaller scopes is because they can be mounted closer to the bore. The 1 ½-inch height shown is typical of many firearm and scope combinations, as well as the airguns employed.

Plotting trajectory at further ranges: A similar but previous test involved just one air rifle. I chose eight identical targets with single bullseyes, but I only shot at seven. The eighth was reserved for the recording of all data. I carefully squeezed off 5-shot groups at 10, 20, 30, 40,

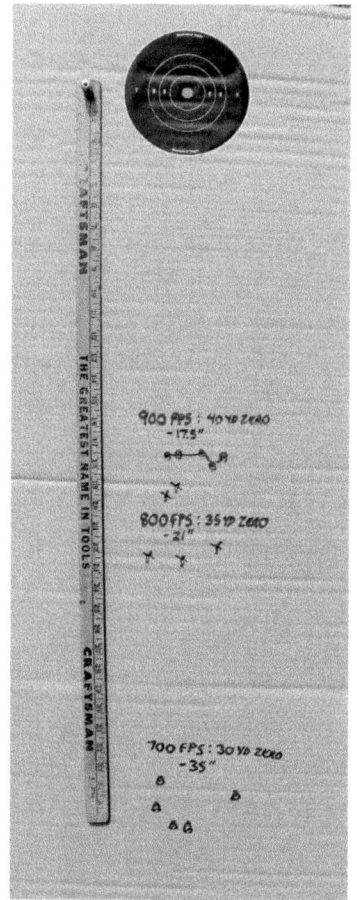

Velocity obviously affects drop. These 100 yard .22 pellet groups were shot while aiming dead-center at the bullseye. A breeze influenced the groups, which is clearly evidenced by the 900 fps series.

A big target is necessary to catch long-range pellet impacts. The bench was moved in 10-yard increments, using a range finder.

50, 60, and even 70 yards, using a clean target for each string along with the same dead center hold.

Since my zippy .22 PCP rifle was zeroed at 40 yards, I knew the three closer groups would probably impact higher. The three further groups would strike lower. The question was, by how much? To find out, I carefully stacked each shot target above the clean one, and then poked a pen through the holes. The bottom target bore no actual strikes, but the marks clearly displayed each impact. As they accumulated, I noted the yardage of each series. Eventually, vertical strips of groups developed from which to mine some data. Especially for those groups shot at closer ranges, the small pen marks were less confusing than a mishmash of holes clustered in close proximity. It was easy to calculate each group's distance above or below the target's center, and that measurement in inches was the amount necessary to hold low or high. I then recorded this information on a small adhesive label and affixed it to the stock. It shows the necessary hold allowances in 10-yard increments out to 70 yards.

Data use: Once a default zero and trajectory is established, very effective field accuracy is possible. With standard crosshairs, you can judge a target's distance and then hold the necessary amount high or low to make hits. Again, having this information readily available is helpful. A rangefinder can really nail things down. As a fairly experienced bow hunter, I normally don't use one afield, but with today's compact laser models it's certainly feasible.

Shooters with ballistic aiming reticles can use them to great effect. Whether mil-dots or holdover lines, the additional aiming points should translate yardages, even if they're oddball. If groups and aiming points don't coincide, try adjusting the magnification. With common domestic 2nd focal plane scopes, this trick will change the relationship of the reticle to the target. At some point, they may match. If the pellet holes are hard to see through the scope, head downrange and highlight each one with black permanent marker. Sooner or later, you may hit a winning combination. At that point, you can use the holdover line for accurate shot placement, although the actual distances may wind up being non-standard.

Another way you could do this is by shooting at objects or targets placed beyond your default zero, while using the holdover lines. You may want to start on maximum magnification, since that's the way these systems are designed to be used. However, it'll more than likely require trial and error. One bonus for mil-dot shooters involves closer targets. Most such reticles have dots on all crosshair sections, so the upper series may work for closer targets – those that require holding low.

Live fire: To illustrate long-range ballistic reticle possibilities, I mounted a Burris 4.5x14 Timberline to my Air Arms M-400 .22 PCP rifle. I used the same scope rings, and I was careful to level the scope's Ballistic-Plex reticle prior to sighting it in. The AA-400 was then carefully registered to the same 40-yard zero used for previous trajectory data. The final two 5-shot groups measured 5/16 & 3/8"; not too shabby!

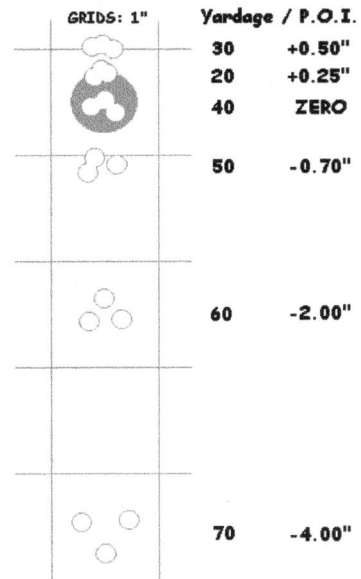

AIR ARMS 400/BURRIS 6X MINI AO
.22 JSB 16.0 Gr. Heavies @ 910 FPS

GRIDS: 1"

Yardage	/ P.O.I.
30	+0.50"
20	+0.25"
40	ZERO
50	-0.70"
60	-2.00"
70	-4.00"

Plotting trajectory can produce useful data from which to calculate hold-points. Note the discrepancy between this chart and previous figures. Many factors can come into play such as velocity, air pressure, temperature, light, and scope height.

Next, it was time to stretch out the distance. An assortment of small steel targets was set up in ten-yard increments, from 40-100 yards. Their surfaces were painted white to show all pellet impacts. I set up a shooting bench and attached a short Harris Bipod to the rifle. Then I grabbed a clipboard and commenced firing. I was busy changing parallax and magnification settings but reliable hits soon appeared. Here's how things shook out with this scope and airgun combination:

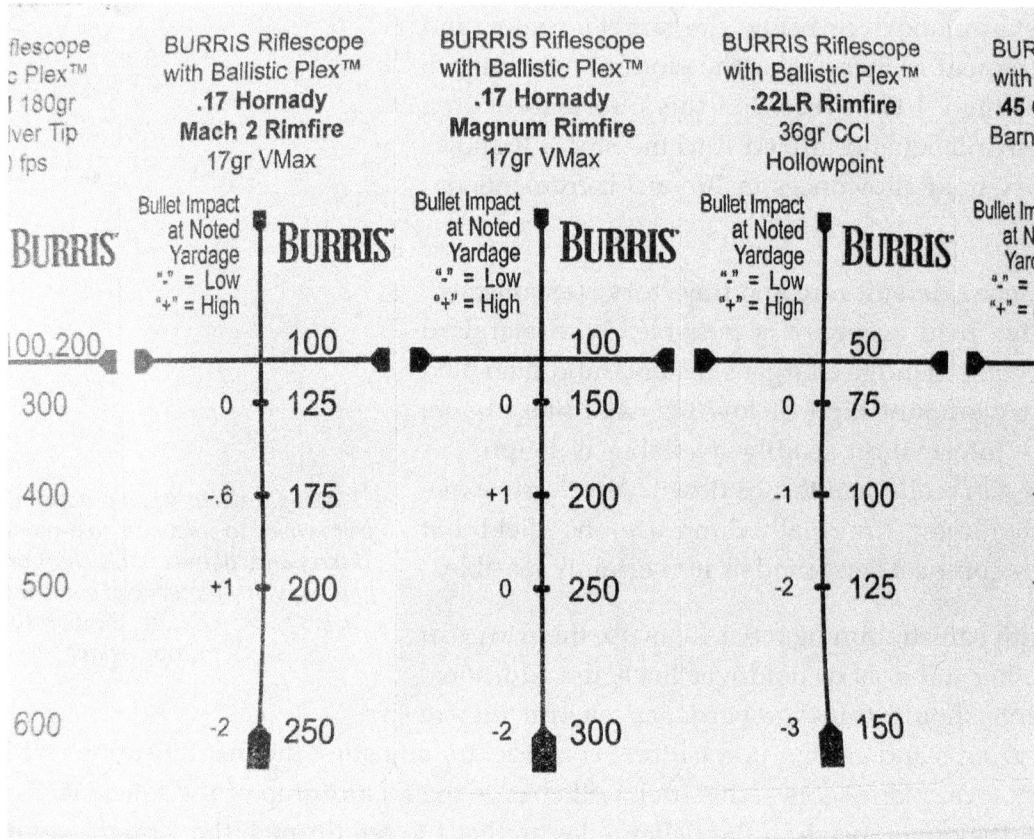

Burris includes a set of handy labels with their Ballistic Plex reticle scopes. Although designed for firearms, the system has airgun applications.

BURRIS BALLISTIC-PLEX LONG-RANGE GUIDE: Drop, hold-over & magnification; 40-yard zero							
Airgun: AA M-400/180 BAR **Scope:** 4.5x14 Timberline AO **Pellet:** .22 JSB 15.9 Gr. /918 fps							
Range	40 **Yd**	50 **Yd**	60 **Yd**	70 **Yd**	80 **Yd**	90 **Yd***	**100 YD**
Drop (inches)	0	-1"	-3"	-6"	-9"	-13"	-17 ½"
B-Plex reticle	Zero	1st	2nd	3rd	3rd	Post	Post
Magnification	N/A	13X	13X	14X	12X	13X	10X
Post: Thick/thin tip of bottom duplex point **90 Yd Alternate: 3rd/ 8 ½ X*							

There are three small hold-over lines below the central crosshairs, followed by a post. A total of five useful aiming points are thus available for aiming purposes. The "post" is really the tip of the lower duplex line, but it will work for our purposes. Changing magnification alters the advertised values of the reticles for alternate uses. Note the 90-yard option, made possible by a power reduction. Dialing from 13X down to 8 ½ X permitted use of the 3rd hold-over point and, while the higher setting may seem better, the coarser post was less precise. At 90 yards, 8 ½ power was still more than adequate for a four-inch steel plate, and the groups tightened up.

To be confident of this data, the entire series was repeated several times on different days. The shooting occurred during calm conditions, and in different light. Five pellets were shot at each target, and all pellet splats were re-painted after each test. The gun was also re-charged often, to help maintain consistency. The furthest ranges really emphasized the effects of decreasing pressure, evident through increased drop. For most purposes, inside 40 yards I can squeak out 45 useful shots, but at 90-100 yards, the precise shot count is less. After around 35 shots vertical stringing began to appear. Those working up their own pre-charged data will want to keep this in mind, along with other variables. The results charted above are based on the performance of one PCP rifle and scope combination. The Ballistic-Plex reticle appears useful, but there are others. Even with published data, the proof will be in the shooting.

Drop beyond 50 yards becomes significant, as does loss of velocity and energy. However, long-range centerfire rifle shooters could convert such data to MOA for scaled down airgun practice.

Airgunners with access to 100 yards might be able to use such dope for scaled down long-range rifle practice. As it turned out here, the 17.5 MOA airgun hold-over was the equivalent of a centerfire 675-yard allowance. That's roughly the elevation we'd need with 168-grain .308 loads, zeroed for 100 yards. Tactical centerfire shooters would probably opt for come-ups but, either way, wind is still in the soup. Being able to reliably tag a small juice can at 100 yards with an airgun has got to translate to great practice. Bore-time is much longer, so follow-through is important. Flight-time seems like an eternity.

Unorthodox aiming: Even with a duplex reticle, there's more to airgun life than just one zero. As mentioned previously, based on the velocity and accuracy of my .22 Air Arms M-400 rifle, it stays zeroed at 40 yards. That's getting out there for an airgun and pellet drop greatly increases beyond that point. At 70 yards, it still has enough punch to tip over pest birds, but pellets strike several inches below the crosshairs. The scope is a 3x9 variable, with a standard duplex reticle and, as it turns out, it also has a second built-in aiming feature. The juncture of the thick/thin lower crosshairs count for *something*, and here's how to figure it out…

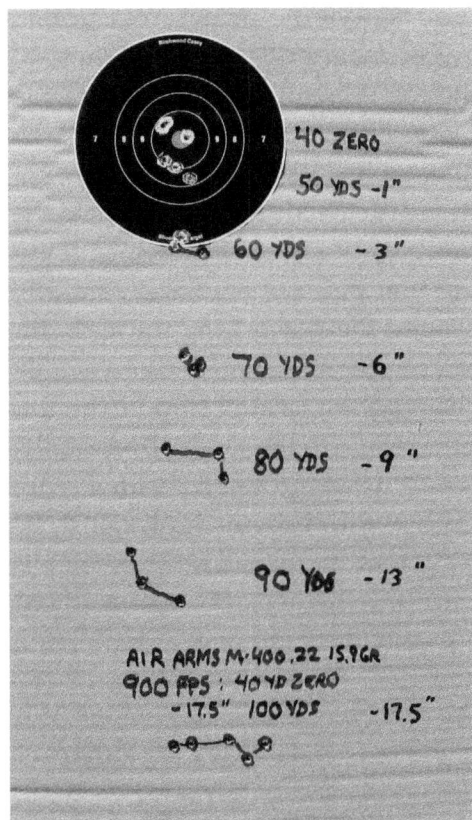

From 70 yards, using an educated guess, I carefully shot 5 pellets at the top edge of a white 8-inch steel plate. The resulting group was easily visible and roughly 4 inches underneath my aiming point. I held the rifle steady on a rest while maintaining that point of aim, and carefully rotated the power ring through different magnifications. This visually changed the relationship of the duplex reticle to the target. Eventually, the 70-yard group coincided with the tip of the bottom duplex post. By luck, that happened at 7X, which is easy to remember. So, even without a true ballistic aiming system, I still had one. By placing the tip of the

Five .22 JSB Diabolo Exacts shot from 85 yards, using a duplex aiming allowance.

thicker lower reticle wire on a 70-yard target, I could hit it - as long as the scope was first set on 7X. Yes, I could just leave it on that power, but a smaller field of view can be difficult to use at closer ranges. At 20 yards, I'd rather shoot on 4X for faster target pickup. Incidentally, as long as the main crosshairs are used, it really doesn't matter what magnification the scope is set on. This assumes it's a decent one that won't wander as power is adjusted. Be sure to check for that condition first.

Turret adjustments? Right about now, everybody's eyes may be glazing over. Some shooters will also think about their turrets. Yes, you can accomplish similar results by adjusting an elevation dial. Not only that, but some math should provide the number of necessary clicks at any reasonable distance. Once everything is sorted out, you can dial in the range and aim dead on. That's the preferred technique for well-trained professional snipers who use high-end equipment. Champion Field Target airgun shooters do the same thing, thanks to well-built optics. With lower-end scopes, adjustments may be less precise and much more subject to wear. It's also possible to get lost on turret revolutions.

For the average airgunner roaming afield, KISS makes sense. That's why I'm sticking with holdover methods. One important thing is needed to make ballistic aiming systems work: level crosshairs. Anyone

Although a target turret will permit dead-on aiming, repeatable adjustments are associated with higher cost optics.

uncertain about the fine points of scope mounting should seek out someone who is. That person might be a gunsmith, who probably won't soak you.

RESEARCH DIVIDENDS

Once equipped with this information, you'll find that hits are possible on small targets throughout the useful range of your rifle. Your scope may permit range compensating adjustments, ballistic reticle aiming, or estimated holds. You can just tape the required hold-off information to the side of your stock. At that point, you'll be prepared to tackle some challenging targets that can economically improve your overall shooting ability.

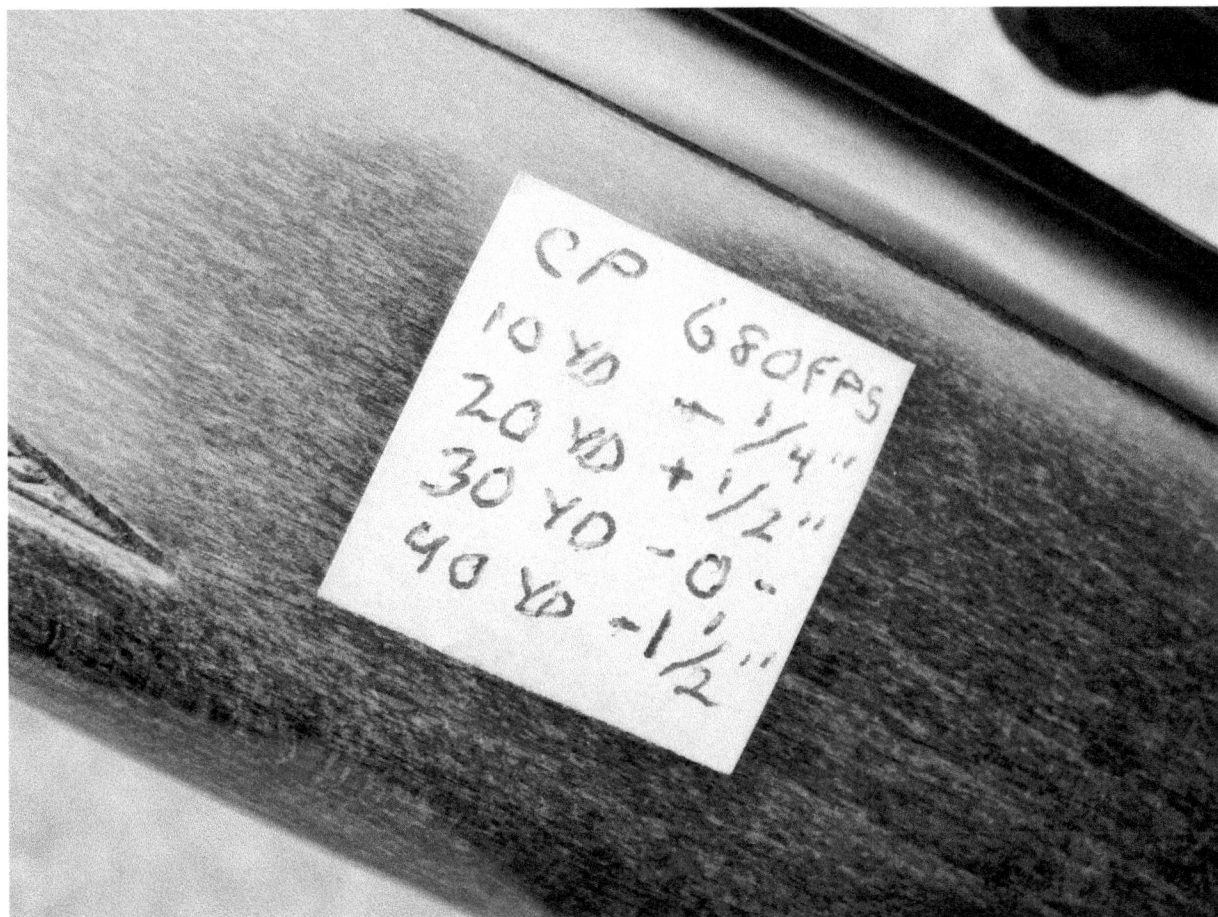

This hold-chart is based on 14.3 grain .22 Crosman Premiers with a 680 fps MV. It's just a small target paster affixed to the side a Beeman R-9.

Now think about how these skills may translate to an accurate long-range rifle setup. You'll already be wired for the basics!

CHAPTER 11

TRAINING TIPS

An airgun makes a great training tool. Many firearm practice drills can be modified or scaled to gain more trigger time. Those requiring fast follow-up shots are out, although a repeating PCP rifle still has value for multiple targets. It can reinforce programming needed to maintain a gun mount during operation of the action.

With a bit of imagination, you can build an entertaining range that will work with all airgun types. It may be situated in a smaller and more accessible spot. The location could even be a garage or basement equipped with a safe backstop. The exact area may dictate the type of shooting activities. Indoors, paper targets will probably be necessary, but they always afford an excellent means to document improvement. So far, no one has come up with a good hole eraser, so excuses are our only recourse when errant holes appear.

Others may have access to a gravel pit or a good-sized piece of vacant land. If a safe area with a proper backstop is available, reactive targets become a possibility. Add some friendly competition and everyone's skills should quickly improve.

FIELD SKILLS

A whole lot of rifle shooters spend way too much time on rests. We've certainly leaned on the process within these pages. But for those chasing dinner, a full-blown shooting bench just isn't in the cards. I'll be among the first to look for some type of makeshift support, whether it's a tree or fence post. Compared to basic stand up (or offhand) shooting, it makes a huge difference. The trouble is, there just might not be anything immediately available. We might have to shoot on our hind legs, and without delay.

Offhand practice: For hunting purposes, a good rifle shot should be able to reliably hit an 8-inch diameter target at 100 yards. There might be an occasional miss, but at least 80% of all shots fired should be hits. Well, that distance is a bit of a stretch for many airguns, but we could certainly scale things down. A 4-inch reactive target, like a round steel plate at 50 yards, makes a dandy .22 rimfire challenge. It will also work with some of the better airguns. Then again, so will a 2-inch target at 25 yards. Suddenly, all of the airguns covered here are in the game. Thanks to air-powered technology, more regular practice will be possible for many of us, without undue expense. Steel targets are fun because they chime out when hit, and can be quickly repainted with an aerosol can. The synthetic spinners are also fun, outside of their safe limitations. Keep at it, and your skills will quickly improve. The ranges can then be stretched out within the practical limits of the gun.

This falling plate rack employs 4" steel resetting targets. Don't forget those shooting glasses!

Other positions: If stability is good (and it is), offhand is the worst position. A lower center-of-gravity helps, and that's where kneeling or sitting come in. Terrain or surroundings may govern the chosen position, but either can be effectively practiced with an airgun. Prone is even better. It can also be tough to practice with spring-powered airguns, due to their significant cocking effort. A pre-charged rifle poses no special challenges, and it's worth trying with either system, assuming you proceed with caution.

Supported field shooting: A clothesline pole or handy tree will work for this shooting. We're trying to gain extra stability through use of some immovable object. Bracing a support hand will greatly reduce offhand tremors. Finding another spot for strong elbow contact provides another quantum leap in stability. Locating both elbows on something like a barrel or rock is even better. All of these techniques can be refined with an airgun, often right in a backyard. Some folks may have shooting sticks on hand. If so, they're worth breaking out for good practice. In essence, they serve as a hand-held bipod, and some like mine even have two legs. One big thing to keep in mind involves hard surface contact with springers.

Opposite-side shooting: If you're right-handed, this means shooting as a leftie. It's not a bad skill to develop, whether defensively or as a hunter. In a serious social situation it's possible to suffer an eye injury resulting from either incoming or outgoing bullet fragments. Those that hit hard cover will likely shed some shrapnel. Lose your dominant-side eye and you'll need to switch shoulders. Some cover scenarios are also better addressed through this approach. As a hunter, I've been able to rescue a few iffy shots by just switching sides. With a hard-kicking firearm, recoil can really ring your chimes during the first few attempts. There are often eye issues that need sorting out. With an airgun, the basics can be more safely sorted out. It's also a fun challenge among other shooters. It'll be weird at first, but you'll soon grasp the basics.

FIELD TARGET COMPETITION

This game is more or less an extension of the field skills covered above, but takes it them to a formalized and competitive level. FT was also briefly touched on in the scope section of Chapter 8. The sport began in the United Kingdom back in 1980, as a means to combine hunting-oriented shooting skills and airgun competition. Shooters progressed through a wooded course, engaging knock-down metal targets representative of typical airgun quarry like squirrels, rabbits, or crows. The game caught on and now has an international governing body: the WFTF, or "World Field Target Federation", which consists of more than 30 member nations. The American Field Target Association sets U.S. rules, and limits

Good ol' fashioned off-hand practice is hard to beat. The gun is a pre-charged BSA. The bolt will be cycled while maintaining a gun mount.

airgun power to 20 ft·lbs of muzzle energy. Targets are set out as far as 55 meters, which is quite a poke, considering their size and the trajectories of the pellets. Like many other shooting disciplines, FT sparked serious equipment not truly practical for real woods use. However, several classes are shot to maintain some degree of normalcy. For those so inclined, Field Target is a real skill sharpener, as well as an opportunity to learn airgun specific technical aspects. Those inclined to try it should choose a gun that can meet the power limits. Thanks to the miracle of the Internet, much more information can be sourced online. New shooters will be welcome, so a visit to a local match is a great starting point.

PRECISION SKILLS

While Field Target certainly falls into this category, there are other less formal venues. Let's say you're into long-range precision shooting with a centerfire rifle. In that case, you'll already have a bipod, rangefinder, and shooting mat. Why not build a scaled-down course that matches the practical limit of your airgun?

Precision paintball madness: Previously, I mentioned shooting at stationary paintballs perched on golf tees. They're not only lots of fun, but can also provide some friendly competition. I've used a ten-foot section of 2x4 drilled with a series of holes. Just plug in wooden golf tees and position a paintball on top of each. They'll explode with centered hits. You can elevate the 2x4 a bit, using

Those who appreciate a challenge can try hitting paintballs at 40 yards.

blocks of wood (or, with trusted shooters, concrete blocks). A few extra holes at each position help, since the tees sometimes get shot off flush with the board.

We shoot .68 caliber paintballs from prone, off a bipod, at around 40 yards. There isn't much room for error, but it's doable with our accurate pre-charged rifles. In fact, sometimes we back out a bit further, which introduces holdover. A fun competition involves eleven targets and two shooters. Each is assigned five paintballs, with an extra designated as a "stop" target. It's off-limits until the first five have been knocked off their tees. The first shooter to clean their set and hit the stop target wins. You can time this for added entertainment. Sometimes the paintballs will topple from a nick, or broken tee. Scoring just depends on how serious you want to be. It helps to remember that shooting is fun!

Scaled-down precision practice, made possible by air-powered bolt-action technology. The centerfire is a .223 Remington Model 700 Compact Tactical and both rifles are perched on Harris bipods.

You really don't need as much magnification as you'd think for reliable hits. I've enjoyed great results on paintballs with an old 6X P/A Burris Scope. I'll occasionally get drafted to perform a high-powered rifle demonstration for our agency's trainees. The targets are golf-balls at 100 yards, shot from prone off a bipod, using a heavy-barreled .308 Remington M-700 bolt-action. Can you see a correlation here? With its scope set on 14X, the value of the airgun drill is clearly evident.

Since springers are hold-sensitive, a bipod is probably out. Prone is tough as well, due to the gymnastics involved with cocking one. However, you can still shoot from other positions, adjusting the range as necessary. Just don't get too close. A low pellet could bounce off the edge of the board. A length of foam pipe insulation may make a safer golf tee base. Paintballs will blow off the tees in a stiff breeze. You can either pre-glue some and face true windage challenges, or just wait for a calmer day.

OTHER FUN TARGETS

Lollipops make a good windproof substitute at further ranges, and Necco Wafers are an old standby. The trick with either is to not eat your targets. A cooler full of ice cubes made from colored water can help to limit consumption.

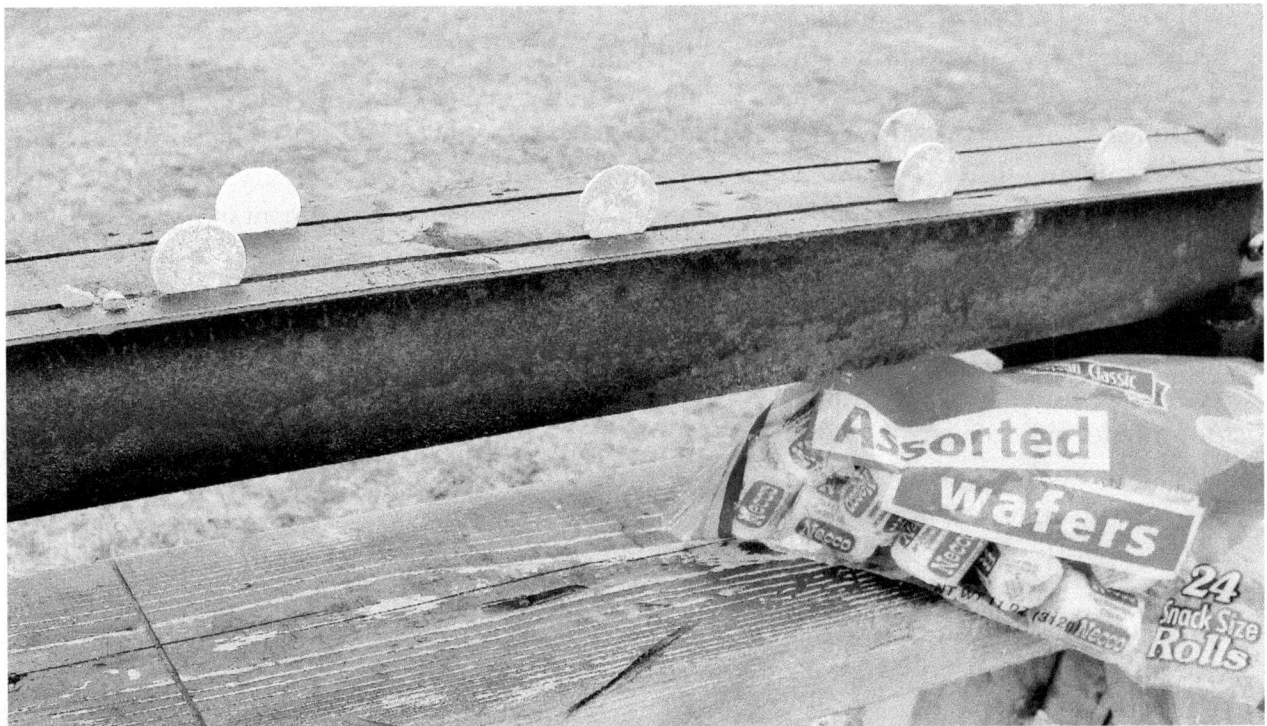

The wooden Necco holder is protected by an angle iron face. Note the pellet impact.

Fired 9mm casings are another option, as described by the late African safari author, Peter Hathaway Capstick. He and a group of acquaintances would partake in a round of "mini-sniping" while shooting precision scoped airguns off of bench rests. Beyond the actual accuracy aspect, elevation and wind allowances must be calculated.

Airgun-rated metal reactive targets are available. Some will reset when an actuating target is properly hit. Regulation "Field Target" silhouettes can be purchased as well. They're shaped like typical airgun quarry as squirrels, rabbits, or birds. A hole in the center of each silhouette displays a small inner plate that represents a kill zone. When solidly hit, the silhouette will topple to indicate an effective field shot. They can be reset using a pull cord. It's worth testing any such targets from further distance, since the more powerful airguns can dent them. Once damaged, they may shoot back! I can't use my .22 PCP rifle on a commercial steel airgun swinger set inside 45 yards.

A high-powered springer will shatter a penny. Some people even blow up marbles, but flying debris is always a concern. Please remember that targets can shoot back, so wear eye protection and think about a safe backstop. In fact, think about *everything*. After that, have fun. Your imagination is the only limit.

HUNTING

I've been doing some pest bird control at a local farm this week. It's late March, with nothing much in season, so the shooting is good practice. The targets are small and fleeting. They present themselves at various angles and distances, demanding a quick but selective response. Broken windows or holes in metal roofs are not good, so situational awareness is essential. In essence, it's a scaled-down shooting decisions and varmint hunt, complete with wind and holdover allowances. Targets could appear from 10 yards out to 50 or beyond. Hits require aiming compensations analogous to those on a quarter mile centerfire course. Wind adds challenges, as does the quest for a stabile position. In this case, I was hugging the edge of buildings or leaning on poultry crates while trying to avoid a herd of curious goats. During the past three trips, I've noticed a distinct improvement in my accuracy and gotten some entertainment, goats aside.

Many states are now allowing use of airguns on some game species. Where legal, an opportunity may exist for a quiet and safe small game outing. It's not only a great way to sharpen up field skills, but also could present an opportunity for access to areas off-limits to firearms. As much as I enjoy hunting gray squirrels with a .22 rimfire, an air rifle does offer some advantages. Sniping squirrels out of trees seems a whole lot safer, thanks to an air gun's limited range. The quiet report also doesn't shake things up as much, permitting multiple shots. Air gun hunting is not only great practice, but also lots of fun!

Reactive steel airgun targets are fun but start at a further distance. These steel swingers were dented by 900 fps .22 pellets at 30 yards.

Well-placed .22 pellets from a 20 ft lb airgun decisively anchored these gray squirrels.

AN UNUSUAL TRAINING REGIMEN

Speed shooting can be a valuable skill. Essentially, it boils down to breaking a shot as soon as the gun hits your face. Rather than precision, this type of shooting is all about relatively close-quarter speed.

As it turns out, an airgun can be a very useful tool for mastery of the basics. It doesn't need to be sophisticated or powerful. In fact, the opposite is beneficial. A basic Red Ryder BB gun will do just fine. If the projectile is slow enough to be seen in flight, that's good! I taught my kids to shoot a shotgun using such a system. I have an old Crosman V-350 BB gun with threaded holes that attach the rear and front

The old Crosman V-350 BB gun point-shooting trainer is hell on tin pie plates.

sights. I unscrewed the rear sight assembly, leaving only the front post. It has a small knob on top that superficially resembles a shotgun bead. Perfect!

We scrounged up a few small aluminum corrugated tins of the type used to package individual pies (yeah, we ate them first). A pie tin was then fastened to a large cardboard box stuffed full of rags located roughly 10 yards down-range. We began with the shooter turned 90 degrees to the target. Starting in port arms with the gun cocked and finger outside the trigger guard, the shooter pivoted on command and quickly mounted the gun. The goal was to break a shot immediately after solid cheek contact was acquired. Total focus was on the target, with both eyes open. The front sight was just a blur, and the gun was pointed rather than aimed. In our case, the stock had been shortened somewhat for a better fit.

If it sounds like the same technique used to engage aerial targets with a shotgun, well, it is! During that discipline, we trust our eyes to steer the gun in the right direction, and our head is actually the rear sight. As long as no eye dominance issues exist, solid cheek contact with the stock will closely index the barrel on the target. Using an airgun as a basic trainer, we can do the same thing. If the BBs can be seen in flight, they'll serve as makeshift tracers. Those that hit the stationary tin will make an audible whack. It won't take long for most shooters to get a handle on the basics, which quickly builds confidence. After several sessions, you can substitute a shotgun and dry-fire at outgoing clay pigeons (or, better yet, incoming targets with a remote-controlled trap). After everything looks right, the odds of a broken clay bird will be high with the first live shell.

This leads back to that Gamo Viper air shotgun. True, you may hit some hand-tossed targets with the little shot shells. Maybe NERF or tennis balls would work. But the ammo isn't cheap, and would be a project to hand-load. Instead, how about using cheap pellets? The gun is laid out like a shotgun with a ventilated rib. It should work well as a natural pointer, for those that can handle its stock. Being synthetic, it would be difficult to shorten, making the whole affair an adult proposition.

LAST THOUGHT ON AIRGUN SHOOTING

The big thing to remember about airguns is that they afford opportunities for extra shooting. If it's nothing more elaborate a bit of informal plinking at spinners or cans, who cares? It's still good practice and a darned good time.

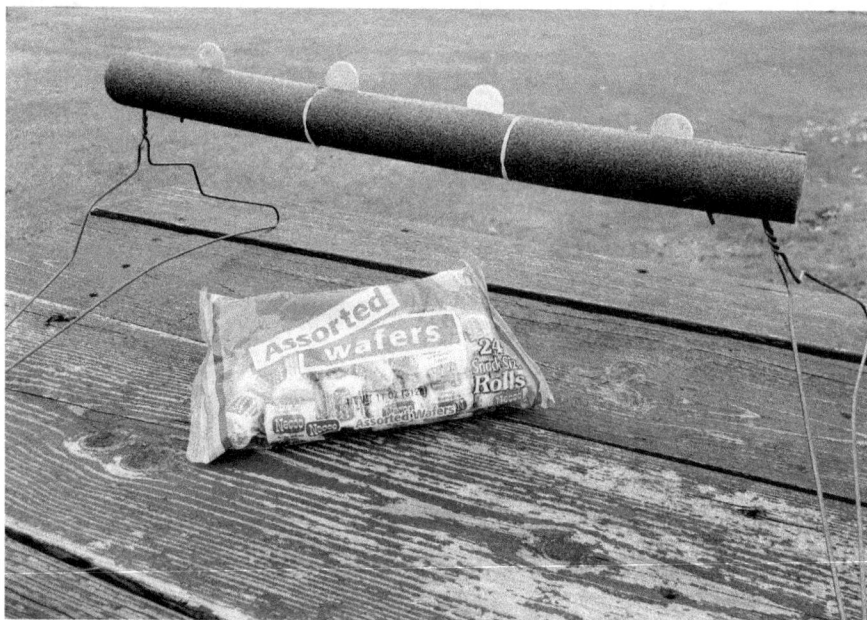

Use your imagination, put on a set of safety glasses, and have fun!

Chapter 12

ACCESSORIES

Many firearms items will serve equally well for airgun uses. A gun case is such an example, and so is a sling. In the case of the latter, quick-disconnect studs will permit its use on multiple guns. Depending on the design of the airgun, you may even be able to share the use of a bipod. A few other handy and reasonably-priced items may prove useful as well.

A gun case offers good protection from dings and dents while helping to maintain your zero. This package will be stowed behind a seat, securely out of sight.

Gun case: There's a good chance many readers already have one. A soft, zippered version will work. Just make sure it will accommodate whatever optical sight is mounted on your rifle. You should be able to pick one up for $35 or less. With careful shopping, you can choose one that will also fit your centerfire rifles. For more money, you can buy a hard shell case, affording greater protection and locking capability. Don't store a gun in a soft case on a long-term basis. The material may accumulate moisture and cause rust to form.

Sling: I often use one is in the woods, where life is a whole lot easier when both hands are free. If your rifles have QD studs, you can transfer a sling as needed in just a few seconds. Some slings are fairly elaborate, but I'm happy with a basic nylon model and QD swivels. It'll be quiet, and it can also be easily dried. My favorite is a "mountain sling", which has sewn-in QD swivels, a thin leather lining in the shoulder area, and 1 ¼" width. The Blackhawk and Butler Creek products run around $20 with swivels. When not in use, I just roll them up, securing the coil with an elastic band. Although a sling is often used as a steadying device with firearms, that role can be problematic for airguns. Springers are a concern that we'll explore next.

Sling studs: One glitch may be the installation of the QD studs on certain airguns. Barrel-cocking spring rifles typically have a slot in their forend at the spot where the front stud would go. In that case, you may be able to attach a barrel-mounted unit. If you look at the HW M-35 shown on the Airguns of Arizona site, you can see such an example. I owned one of these elegant rifles, and the system worked fine for carrying purposes. A barrel-mounted stud won't permit sling-tensioned shooting, though. Such force could change your zero, or even pop the barrel open. Positioning the hardware closer to the breech will reduce the chance of that during shoulder carry. I still wouldn't use this system without a very positive barrel locking detent. A bipod is out, which is pretty much a moot point on a springer anyway. Uncle Mikes sells barrel band sets. Any standard rear wood screw stud should mount to the butt stock. Some shooters use a barrel band on underlever guns, building up the cocking arm with layers of electrical tape. Success would depend on how well the arm was secured, and I'd want it as close to the forend as possible.

Sling studs will permit the convenient use of a sling or bipod. This mountain sling has QD swivels and can be reattached to a secondary bipod mounting point.

A pair of threaded stock studs went on my PCP rifle without any trouble, and the front one also served as a bipod attachment. Just remember to remove the stock before drilling commences! Creating a hole in the air reservoir of your pet pre-charged rifle would be both exciting and disappointing. If in doubt, pay a gunsmith to install the studs. Cost should be fairly reasonable, and they'll probably be centered to boot.

Air Force sells mounting hardware for their guns. You could probably jury-rig a Marauder Pistol. A pump-up rifle is probably better off if left as is.

Bipod: I don't normally roam afield with one, but it makes a great training aid. Hook one on an accurate rifle, and you can learn how to master bipod techniques on reduced-scale targets. A pre-charged gun is the most practical candidate, assuming sling studs are present. I like the folding-leg Harris bipods, which are well-proven designs. Mine have seen much use on firearms and, on my PCP .22 air rifle, point of impact isn't affected in the least.

The Harris base attaches to a QD sling stud, using a simple tension screw. It houses two spring-loaded folding legs, and several different heights are offered. Each has telescoping leg sections to permit additional extension with precise adjustments. My favorite is their HBMLS with 9-13" notched leg stops and a swivel feature. A less expensive model is sold without the swivel feature, and friction-knob leg locks. It's also harder to adjust from prone. The shortest 6-9" model will work for many folks. It's a bit too low for me, making it a bench affair. Mine sees much less use than the all-around 9-13" version. Cost is around $100, but it can be used on a number of different rifles. In fact, that's the beauty of the design.

Precision paintball sniping technology. A shooting mat is nice, but not essential.

Shooting rests: The same bench equipment listed in *Rimfire Rifles: A Buyer's and Shooter's Guide* will work for many airguns. I employ the same tripod and sandbag arrangement used for bench rest work with rimfire and centerfire rifles. The system really consists of five key pieces, if you count a sturdy shooting bench, a chair, adjustable metal rest, sandbag, and extra rear bag. Stability, proper orientation, and comfort are crucial. This excerpt from *Rimfire Rifles* might help:

"You can spend several hundred dollars on a top-end, fully adjustable, heavy-cast tripod with fitted bags. We maintain a Wichita unit on our range, along with several sandbags. It's made from a heavy casting, and has pointed screw-adjustable feet at the end of each low tripod leg. A central threaded stem adjusts to various heights using a large thumbwheel. A metal cradle on top holds an eared leather sandbag for proper forend support. A separate larger-eared bag is positioned at the rear of the shooting bench to cradle the rifle's stock. Once properly set up, rock-steady support can be maintained. That takes most of the human equation out of serious accuracy testing. Caldwell sells a similar but more reasonably-priced unit for less than $130. It's called 'The Rock Shooting Rest & Rear Bag Combo', which comes range-ready with both bags."

Caldwell Stable Table, with "The Rock Rest" set up for PCP rifle testing. Note the forend stop and rear sling stud, located for consistent results.

A pre-charged air rifle isn't fussy at all about rest contact. Springers are a different story. As we've discussed, they tend to be hold-sensitive, so standard firearm bench rest techniques won't work. Spring gun shooters may be better off with a couple of pillows instead of a tripod rest. I still use the latter, but cover it with a few layers of towel. I then position my support hand between the rifle and rest.

Cleaning kit: Airguns don't need frequent cleaning, but eventually, the bore will probably accumulate gunk. Depending on the type of airgun, your firearms gear may work. The solvents and wire brushes are out, but a .17 HMR rod will work just fine on a .177 bore. A rod that will clean a .22 caliber barrel will work on .22 or .25 caliber airgun. The same patches and jags (or loops) are fine. I much prefer a one-piece rod to prevent damage from sectioned edges.

Many airgun designs require some sort of pull-through system like the Otis kit. It's handy to tote, since the cable can be coiled up and stored in the small supplied accessory case. Cost is around $30. Special airgun lubricants will be needed to prevent violent combustion. We'll look more closely at them in the airgun maintenance chapter.

Rangefinder: Prices have come down to the point where many of these laser-powered units are fairly affordable. Some readers may already own one for use as hunters. The archery units are fairly compact, and will work within airgun distances. My Bushnell 1500 ARC is a longer-range unit that has served me well. It's since been replaced by some similar variations. I don't use a rangefinder all that often with an airgun, but it's great in some situations. One example is during setup of targets to figure out trajectories. It meshes nicely with the next instrument...

Chronograph: Just about everyone is interested in the actual velocity of their airgun. The way to find out is to shoot some pellets through one of these instruments. Actually, you'll be a whole lot happier if you shoot them *over* it.

A laser rangefinder can be a useful tool for numerous shooting disciplines. One 9-volt battery will power this tried and true Bushnell unit for a very long time.

Most work off two sensors that "see" a projectile and calculate the time it takes to traverse the gap. Projectiles are carefully fired above the sensors, parallel with the top of the instrument. Most units then display the velocities on an LED screen that faces the shooter. Prices have become quite reasonable. The battery-powered "Competition Electronics ProChrono Digital" is a simple, self-contained unit that only costs $100. A threaded socket on its bottom will mount the instrument to a camera tripod. Once set up, it will record data from a series of shots and display each one in feet per second, average velocity, etc.

Be prepared for psychological trauma after shooting your "1200 FPS" springer through one. Pump-up shooters may have fun seeing what speeds various strokes generate. The PCP crowd will likely discover a sweet pressure range for the most consistent velocities. A chronograph will also work with bullets and arrows.

So much for 820 fps, as claimed by the manufacturer. The Competition Electronics chronograph clearly disagrees!

Tip: If you borrow one, have its owner do the shooting. Low hits are all bad. Done it, been there.

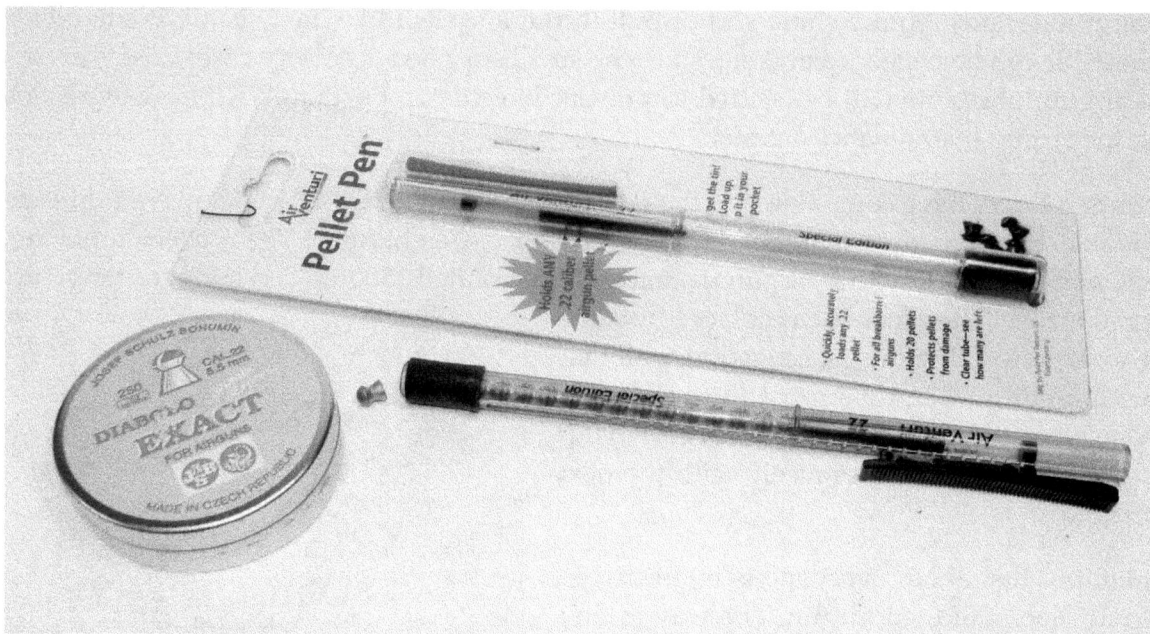

Air Venturi's Pellet Pens are handy little gadgets – especially with barrel-cockers.

Pellet Pen: This aptly-named device has a transparent body, and is used to dispense pellets. It's really designed for use with break-barrel springers. Just orient the tip behind the breech and push a small tab. A pellet will emerge from the pen-sized body, aligned with the bore. With a bit of extra finesse, it's also possible to dispense a pellet into the single-shot breech of some bolt-action pump-up or pre-charged rifles. The .22 version holds 15 standard pellets and, since my PCP rifle delivers 45 useable shots, I have three. Handling an open container of small projectiles almost guarantees spillage, so for $10, the Pellet Pen is a useful little gizmo.

Extra magazines: PCP repeaters could benefit from at least one spare. Better yet, why not buy enough to approximate the number of useful shots from your gun? When the last one is empty, it's time for more air. That beats counting individual shots, and you won't be fiddling with loose pellets while afield. The Marauder magazines run around $15. As a minimum, I'd want two. That way, you can keep shooting while reloading an empty one. With a bit of practice, a Pellet Pen also works on empty magazines. They should be carried in a manner that will keep them free of pocket lint or other debris that could infiltrate the rifle.

Single-shot tray: Marauder rifle owners may want to pick up one of these. It fills the magazine opening and serves as a guide to assist insertion of a single pellet. A slight increase in accuracy may be seen, due to less pellet deformation. I use one at times with my Air Arms PCP repeater. In fact, I leave it right in the gun during storage. I keep a pair of pre-loaded magazines within reach, stored separately from the rifle. Once I start shooting, I'll just pluck out the single-shot tray and exchange it for a magazine. Worse case, if I do leave the house without a magazine, the gun will still be operational. The orientation of pellets in the single-shot tray is a bit tricky, but it works. Cost for the Marauder unit is $18.

Reactive targets: The same steel types that work with .22 rimfires are fun with airgun pellets (but not BBs!). The self-sealing synthetics might cause trouble with pellets, so read and follow the cautions. Some can shoot back with low-velocity airgun projectiles.

Eye and ear protection: One nice thing about most airguns is their mild report. A bare-barreled, high-powered PCP rifle might have a loud enough snap to justify indoor hearing protection, but it probably won't be necessary with other types of airguns. On the other hand, eye protection is important. Pellets or BBs can bounce off surfaces that would be penetrated by bullets.

You probably won't need hearing protection (at least, not outdoors), but shatter-resistant safety glasses are essential airgun gear.

Champion Target's hinged pop-up model is spring loaded. You can assemble a fun array and touch them up with spray paint.

CHAPTER 13

CLEANING, MAINTENANCE AND STORAGE

Overall, the airgun cleaning process isn't much different from firearm procedures. Much of the gear used for firearm maintenance should work, BUT there are a few major exceptions! You can get in serious trouble with the wrong lubricants, and bronze bore brushes should be avoided.

Airguns don't need frequent cleaning, but they'll still need *some* maintenance. One thing we can't do is mindlessly spray solvents or lubricants like WD-40 into the gun. While the linkages and internals of springers need periodic attention, the right lubes are essential. Multi-stroke pneumatics are a bit less fussy, but still in the same boat. The pre-charged pneumatic guns contain fewer moving parts, but their high operating pressures raise other concerns. The exterior surfaces of all types should be wiped down after handling, and their barrels may need occasional attention.

SAFETY

First, the obvious: inspect your gun carefully to ensure it is unloaded! Then, do it again. A set of safety or shooting glasses is worth wearing for protection from solvent splatter or flying parts. When the job is finished, be sure to wash up thoroughly. Lead exposure is no joke and, besides direct ingestion, residual lead can be inadvertently deposited on furniture and clothing. This is a real concern for anyone with kids.

BARREL CLEANING

Eventually, the bores of all airgun types will accumulate some gunk. It will likely be a deposit of lubricant and lead, but believe it or not, combustive residue may also exist. Depending on the type and quantity of oil, a spring gun can actually "diesel" when shot. One good clue is a bit of smoke and the unmistakable odor. A small amount of dieseling is not unusual, but it can gradually deposit combustive byproducts in a barrel. A decline in accuracy is good indication of fouling. When possible, we should clean any barrel from breech to muzzle. It's also not a bad idea to clean the bore of a PCP gun with the rifle inverted. That helps prevent any errant solutions from entering the air transfer port.

Cleaning Rods: The easy fix with .22 break-barrel springers is to just use your rimfire rod. Avoid the jointed types though. They pick up debris, which can score a relatively soft airgun barrel. In fact, some of the pump-up guns are made from brass. A stainless steel or coated one-piece rod is a wise all-purpose investment. Its threaded tip will accommodate essential items like patch jags or loops.

I don't use a standard bore brush in an airgun barrel. Patches are a safer bet, and copper fouling is normally not much of an issue. Without extra care, it's sometimes possible to dislocate the O-ring breech seal on some guns.

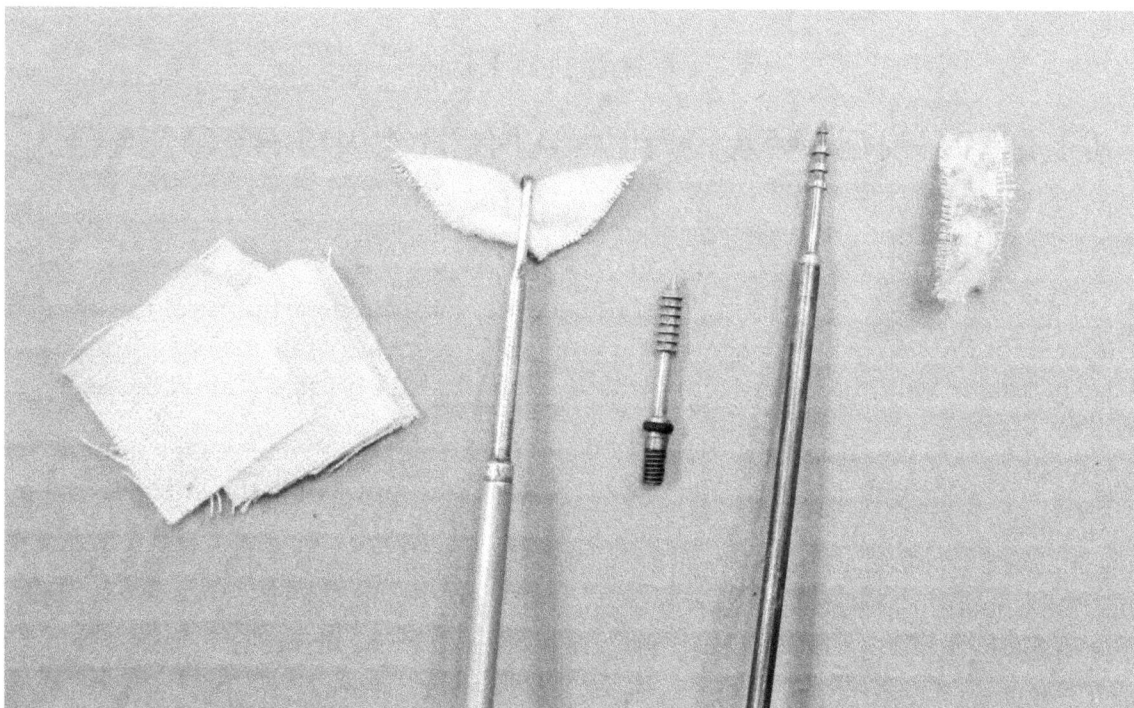

The .22 and .17 caliber rods will work with firearms or airguns. Note the absence of a bore-brush.

A cleaning rod won't work with under or side lever guns for breech-to-muzzle cleaning. Most bolt-action types, whether pump-up or PCP guns, share the same problem. Their bolts interface with a striker, and can't be easily removed. A simple fix is a flexible pull-through barrel cleaning system.

Flexible systems: You just need a way to snake it through the barrel until the accessory end protrudes through the action. At that point, a patch can be attached and the cable can be pulled through the bore. This sounds easy until you try it with a shrouded barrel. Normally, the actual barrel is shorter than its external sleeve. It's also smaller in diameter. Unlike a rigid rod, a flexible cable will want to curl off the axis of the bore. This misalignment may cause it to hang up inside the cap on a shroud after it clears the barrel. I insert a plastic soda straw into the muzzle of my PCP rifle's shroud until it contacts the barrel. Then I feed the cable through the open breech.

A pull-through kit is a handy item to keep on hand. It's portable and will provide a means to clean the barrels of various airgun designs.

It'll remain centered as it enters the straw, and when it emerges from the muzzle, you can pull the pre-patched cable through without cussing too badly. Some people use monofilament fishing line, but it can score a muzzle without very careful handling.

Cleaning pellets: Picture little felt "pellets", which can be shot through your barrel. With spring guns, you'll want to fire a couple per shot just to ensure adequate back pressure. Otherwise, you may cause the same kind of damage that could happen from dry-firing. Be sure to wear safety glasses, and point your muzzle in a safe direction. They won't travel far, but cleaning pellets start out at very high velocity. Besides concerns about close-range injuries, a strike to the internal baffles of a shrouded airgun may result in damage. They're not essential, but some people use them periodically in spring guns.

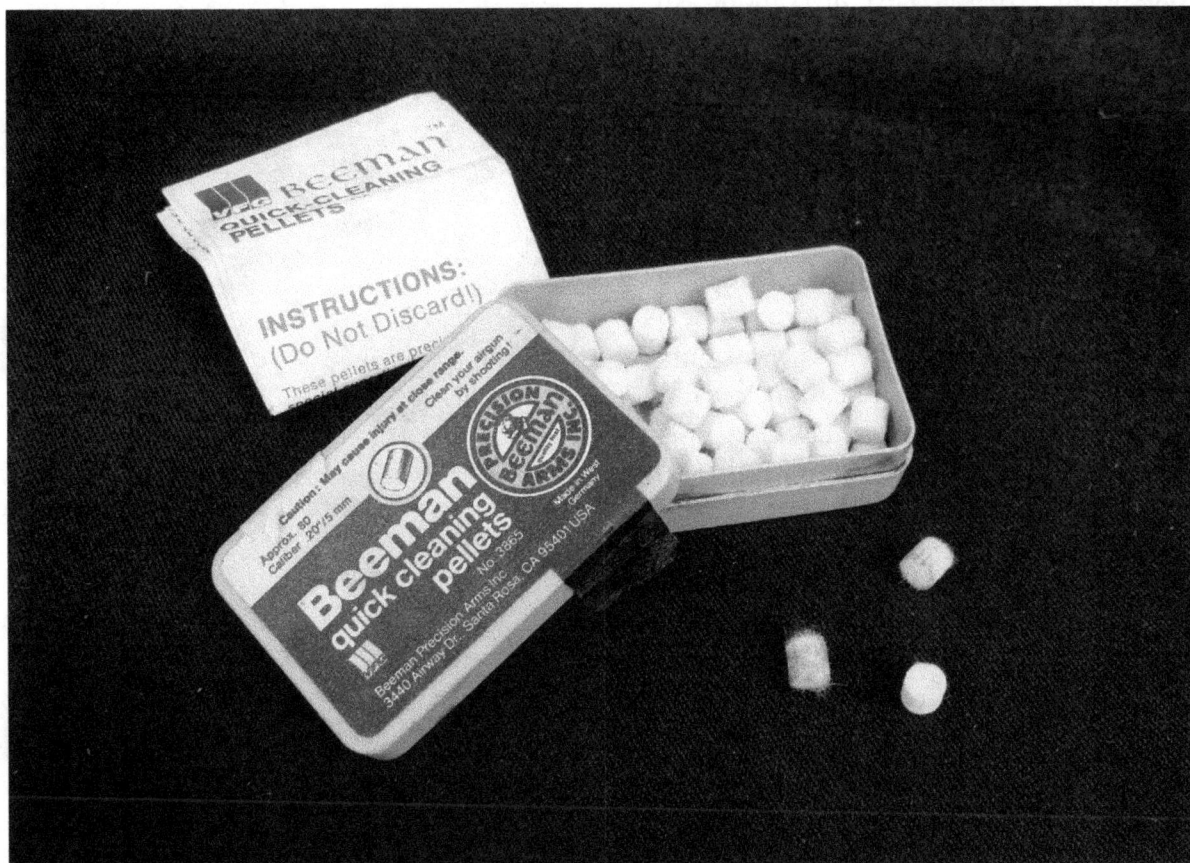

Bore cleaning made easy. They're not the ultimate solution, but cleaning pellets will capture some crud. Always load two in spring guns for piston cushioning.

When to clean? I don't touch the barrel of my PCP rifle until it has digested at least 250 pellets. A small amount of Break-Free on a couple of pull-through patches is all it takes to remove a thin black layer of pellet lube and lead. If accuracy starts to fall off, this is a good starting point. Some high-velocity PCP owners lubricate their pellets to minimize lead deposits. I haven't found this extra step beneficial, perhaps because of well-finished rifling. It's not uncommon to find plenty of glop in the bore of a new gun, especially a springer. A few careful passes with a patch should wipe it clean.

LUBRICANTS

Most airgun manufacturers sell their spring guns with generous lubrication. The theory is that many users won't understand or take the time to perform periodic maintenance. Actually, without a basic understanding of such designs, they're better off untreated. The wrong lubricants can damage seals, or even ignite under pressure. Too much isn't good, either. Because many spring guns come heavily lubricated right from the factory, you may notice some dieseling. It has an unmistakable odor, and a slight trace of smoke inside the barrel may be evident as well. This condition should diminish as shooting progresses, and the gun may also smooth out. Peak operation may not occur until around 1000 shots. At that point, the moving parts *may* need some attention.

A professional I trust is Steve at Pomona Airguns. His advice is to not mess with the innards of spring guns. He says the reputable manufacturers have gone to durable synthetic piston seals that just don't need much maintenance. This is a more recent development. Those shooters with older guns may be running on leather seals that will eventually dry out. Some of the first-generation synthetic springer seals weren't all that durable. In the end, your gun's behavior may tell you if lubrication is called for. The development of a squawking noise during cocking is a sure indication of the need for lube.

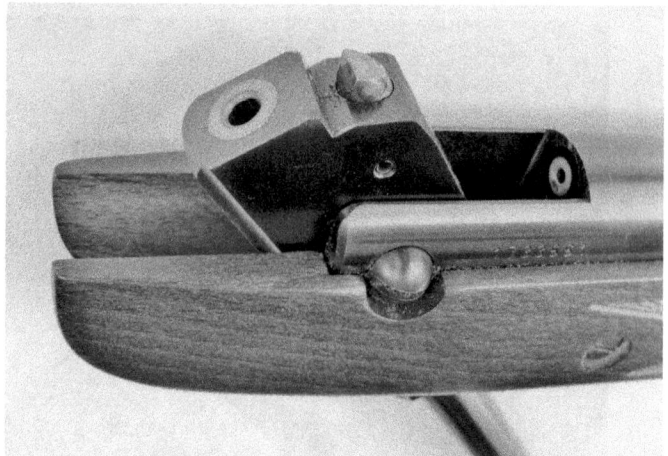

Bore and breech seal access is easy with a barrel-cocking springer. The locking stud and screws should be periodically lubed. Check the screws for tightness, too.

Choices: The springers will need two specialty tubes: a high flash point air chamber lubricant ($15) and a spring/linkage lube ($13). You can also buy them as part of an airgun kit for a bit more. RWS will advise you to apply only two drops of air chamber lube after each series of 1000 shots. An application needle inserted through the airport makes this easy. A few pellets shot afterwards will help distribute the oil.

Application: Spring oil can handle lubrication of the other moving parts, such as the barrel pivot area, cocking linkage, and mainspring. The latter can be accessed through the cocking slot underneath the gun. Each area only requires a drop or two. Too much will just attract dirt or debris, which can accelerate wear. The

The air hole of this pump-up rifle looks like a good spot for oil, but it's really an inlet.

exterior metal surfaces can be wiped down with a very light coating of the same oil to prevent corrosion. Just like a firearm, a simple wipe should occur after each handling.

Again, penetrating or acid-type oils and firearm solvents are no good. Petroleum-based lubricants should never come in contact with the fill area of a pre-charged gun! The Marauder manual will advise the application of some silicone chamber oil on the breech O-ring after every 500 shots. A bit of moly graphite grease will keep the bolt running smooth. These steps will also work with pump-up guns, but don't forget to maintain their linkages.

CO2 guns will leak without regular lubrication. Crosman recommends applying a drop of "Pellgunoil" to the threads of the piercing tube cap after every 250 shots. A drop on the neck of each new cartridge is also advised. These steps will help maintain the integrity of the seals and prevent the loss of gas.

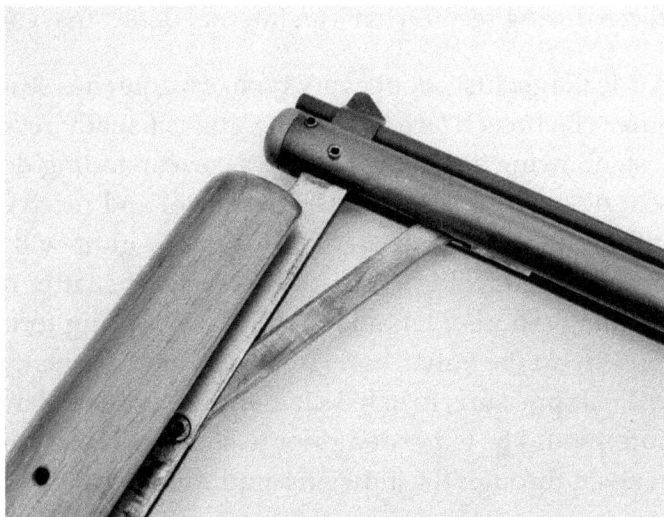

Moving parts do need lubrication. Occasional attention to this linkage will greatly extend the life of the gun.

Good stuff for pump-up and CO-2 powered guns.

OTHER CONCERNS

Loose screws: The vibration of spring guns can loosen stock-mounting fasteners, the barrel hinge points, and scope mounts. Accuracy will begin to deteriorate, and groups may also shift. The stock on pneumatic guns is often only secured with one stock bolt, which can gradually loosen during use. If you detect some movement, it's time to snug things up. A gunsmith screwdriver kit is worth owning. It will come with a nice assortment of hollow-ground blades to match nearly any screw found on a firearm or airgun. Each bit inserts into a driver shank, where it is magnetically retained. Switching them out only takes a few seconds, so it's usually easy to achieve a properly fitting screw and bit combination. Brownell's is a great source for these kits. The standard carpenter screwdrivers are almost guaranteed to bugger up gun screws.

Scope movement: A wandering zero is a good indication that something is loose. This is a frequent problem with magnum-power spring guns. If everything appears all right on the rifle, check the scope mount hardware. Also check for any ring movement on the receiver's mounting grooves, plus creeping of the scope within the rings. The optical system will act like a body at rest during recoil. A spring gun will surge forward upon discharge, and the scope system will try to move rearward. If everything seems in order, the scope itself may be suspect. The lower-priced types may jump a few clicks during recoil. That's an internal defect that can drive you nuts. It's common with cheap scopes.

Air leakage: Just about every type of airgun has seals, and their integrity is necessary to contain pressure. The breech face of a spring gun is usually recessed for an O-ring. It may deteriorate or even be lost, allowing air to escape with a corresponding decrease in velocity. You can often check a suspect seal by cupping a hand over the barrel and receiver junction during discharge. A feather or tuft of milkweed works even better. Pneumatic guns will have a small O-ring seal on the end of their bolt probe or just inside their barrel breech. The latter type is susceptible to loss or damage during bore cleaning. Those who tinker with striker spring force can cause gradual depressurization from extra tension on the valve. Foreign objects are the enemy of all pneumatic systems which are best stored with air pressure, to help seat their valves against dust. CO2 systems are just the opposite. Their pressure should be expended prior to storage. These guns, along with pump-up types, can sometimes be revived through the judicious application of the correct lubrication.

Broken spring: Loss of tension or an unusual noise during cocking can indicate a failure in a springer. At that point, quit shooting to prevent scoring of the air chamber. The gas piston guns can suffer a similar failure from a worn seal. For most folks, this situation will require service from a qualified source. Remember, a springer with enough power to meet survival needs will have a very stout mainspring.

Springers generate lots of vibration and recoil. A sudden zero change means it's time to check for loose scope mounting screws. On the other hand, that receiver end-cap is under lots of pressure even when the gun is un-cocked. Don't mess with it.

Disassembly: In most spring-powered systems, the mainspring remains partially compressed even when uncocked. As mentioned in the Airgun Safety chapter, we're better off leaving disassembly to those who are equipped with the correct tools and knowledge. The most powerful springers can violently disassemble as their end cap is removed. Getting everything back together afterwards is a real project. Some people use a furniture clamp with padded jaws, gradually relieving the end cap pressure on mid-powered spring guns. Then again, a little bit of knowledge can produce regrettable results. This applies to the other airgun systems as well. They need to be completely depressurized before servicing, *with the correct parts and lubes.*

Tunes: Some dedicated airgun owners put extra effort into enhanced performance of their guns. Spring guns are sometimes disassembled and stripped of their heavy factory lubricants. The air cylinder and piston are then polished for smooth travel. A replacement spring may also be installed, along with high-performance lubricants. The goals are smooth cocking, minimal vibration, and extra velocity. The PCP crowd sometimes plays with air transfer ports of varying diameters and different valve striker springs. These modifications are best performed by knowledgeable custom airgun tuners. The Internet is a great source for such services, as well as general airgun information, both good and bad!

STORAGE

Exterior: After using your airgun take a few moments to wipe down its metal surfaces with a protective layer of oil. It won't take much. You can apply a thin film with something like Breakfree or Rem Oil, using a cloth. I keep one in a Tupperware container, located on top of my gun safe. After a while, the cloth will absorb enough oil to maintain itself with only periodic renewal of lube. Any guns placed in long-term storage should be periodically checked for signs of rust or corrosion.

Scope lens caps are a great investment. They'll ward off bad weather and protect the lenses from dust.

Scope: A set of lens caps is a wise investment. They'll not only ward off water or dust, but also solvents and oils. The best way to clean the lenses is to blow them off. That won't always work, so a "Lens Pen" is a wise investment. You *can* clean a lens with caution by misting its surface with a breath, followed by gentle attention and a very soft cleaning patch or eyeglass clothe. Just remember that the special anti-reflective coatings are very thin. Don't mess with any screws in the scope. It's a sealed unit, and disassembly will ruin it.

Airgun bolts are not easily removable, so checking for a clear barrel requires other techniques.

Check it! Double-check any type of gun before putting it away. We need to be certain that it's unloaded. A barrel-cocking springer is easy enough to inspect. Just pop the barrel open far enough to look through the breech end. Other types, like side or underlever spring guns, can be tougher. Sometimes, the easiest method involves loading a pellet and then immediately shooting it into a safe backstop. A length of 3/16" dowel can be used as well. I make it a point to shoot any pneumatic guns before entering my living space. At that point, it remains uncocked with its safety on. You can dry-fire a pneumatic, which isn't a bad last minute precaution as long as a safe backstop is at hand. I have occasionally pointed one at the thick dog bed beside the gun safe before pulling the trigger (no, the dog is not in it).

Springs and pressurization: Remember, we don't want to dry-fire a spring gun. However, it shouldn't be stored cocked, either. The same rule of thumb applies to all other airgun types, where cocking will generally involve a bolt or lever. Long-term compression of springs will result in their loss of tension. On the other hand, pneumatic guns should be stored with some pressure. PCP types will be fine at any reading. The pump-up guns can get two or three strokes. In either case, air pressure will help maintain valve seating to seal out dust. The rule of thumb with CO2 guns is to completely depressurize them when done shooting.

Note: Whatever system is involved, please make darned sure the gun is unloaded! Then, store it responsibly.

SECURITY

The following excerpt from *Shotguns: A Comprehensive Guide* applies equally well to other firearms, as well as airguns:

"Periodic inspections and basic cleanings go a long way towards peace of mind, and will also help maintain your investment. The means of storage is equally important. External corrosion can appear in a surprisingly short amount of time and, if undiscovered, it can cause pitting and permanent damage. Long-term gun case storage may result in transfer of moisture from padded surfaces, which can accumulate humidity. Besides gun cases, wrapping a gun in cloth can wreak havoc, even if stored indoors. Any damp place like a basement or shed is just as bad.

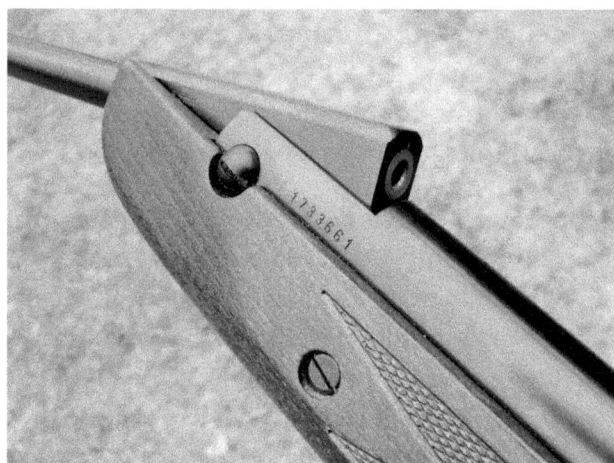

You can safely inspect the breech of many springers without cocking the gun.

That's why a good gun safe located in a dry and stable environment is worthwhile. Desiccant packs and dehumidifier rods should provide adequate protection from rust if some thought goes into the final location. I haven't had any issues using a safe alone, which is located in a primary living space. The extra peace of mind afforded by a good safe is another major dividend. The *Survival Guns* edition covers safes and other storage options in detail. We all have an obligation to ensure that our firearms and ammunition don't fall into the wrong hands. A locked case or trigger-lock may deter kids or honest folks, but are really just interim steps."

Sources: Brownell's and Midway USA carry a large selection of general gun cleaning gear and solvents. In addition to their catalog, Cabela's has a number of walk-in retail locations for some hands-on shopping. Your local gun shop is worth a visit as well. Since some also provide gunsmith service, a good customer relationship can prove valuable.

Your gun's manual is a good first step for specific information! Pyramyd Air offers free access to many on their website. Click on a specific airgun model, and you'll often see a link.

CHAPTER **14**

CONCLUSION AND AIRGUN SOURCES

There are just some things I wouldn't want to be without. A good set of binoculars, a rangefinder, and serviceable outdoor clothing come to mind. Besides a collection of firearms, an airgun also makes the short list. It fills a niche, despite the fact that I live in a rural area. While I can (and sometimes do) shoot firearms in my backyard, I feel much more comfortable with air-powered technology. Errant shots, although unlikely, are of much less concern. So is noise. The sound of an airgun pellet hitting a steel target is often louder than the actual report from the gun. And, even the light projectiles from my relatively potent PCP rifle quickly run out of steam, which limits their maximum carrying distance.

Do you need an airgun? It's really an individual question. Many readers no doubt live in urban areas where the discharge of any gun is taboo. An airgun provides the means for some discreet shooting right inside a home. An impromptu "range" can be constructed in a basement, where what little noise exits can be minimized. Board up any windows and projectile containment is assured. I wouldn't feel as comfortable with any sort of .22 rimfire, including a "lowly" CB Cap. I'll occasionally shoot some in my basement, but not while anyone else is home. They have enough punch to possibly penetrate a floor or exterior wall. A more substantial backstop will be necessary, and ventilation will be a concern. Their heavier bullets strike my steel bullet trap with an audible clang, while producing harmful lead dust. These issues are largely mitigated through use of an airgun.

Such concerns won't matter as much outdoors, but projectile containment is still a major issue. You really can't safely shoot .22 Shorts or CB Caps in any type of residential setting. In fact, you may not be able to shoot an airgun either. Even in a safe area, some nervous neighbor could complain. However, one saving factor may be the defense that "it's only an air gun". The types we examined are certainly not run-of-the-mill BB guns, but most laypeople probably won't know the difference. Somehow, airguns still maintain social acceptance not only domestically, but around the globe. As a result, we benefit from sophisticated designs capable of outstanding performance. Accuracy can be phenomenal, and thanks to a quiet report with useful power, true stealth performance is ours for the taking. The ability to access some very tight places suddenly becomes a reality.

If society completely falls apart, the need for food will become paramount. At that point, clandestine hunting may be necessary, and an airgun may be just the right tool. In urban areas, a railroad underpass or abandoned factory full of pigeons could provide some hope of nourishment. Less densely populated areas may host squirrels or other animals that could be unobtrusively harvested. Get hungry enough, and even song birds will have appeal. Resorting to this wouldn't make my day, it but would sure beat trying to eat an Audubon manual. If you recall, there is an old song about blackbird pie.

Meanwhile, as we wait for the apocalypse that will hopefully come later, why not sharpen up our shooting with a bit of airgun practice? Thanks to inexpensive pellets, we can enjoy some low-impact entertainment. While rimfire ammo has been in short supply, airgun pellets are still plentiful. In fact, we can mail-order both airguns and their ammunition, which don't fall under the jurisdiction of BATF (check your local regulations).

Still, all firearm safety rules will need to be followed. The airguns we've examined are certainly not toys. Handle them carefully, and expand your shooting horizons.

AIRGUN PRODUCT AND INFORMATION SOURCES

With apologies to the many other great sources not shown, the following is but a short list of well-known airgun dealers and information providers. Dealer websites are often a great source for in-depth information about specific products. Some also have handy calculators to determine things like the number of fills off a scuba tank, velocity to foot-pounds conversion, etc.

The more generalized airgun sites can link you into all sorts of fascinating places. Among them are airgunsmiths specializing in tuning, unusual accessories, gun stock upgrades, and heavy customization.

AIRGUN DEALERS

The first four listings are those that I'm most familiar with. They can be found on the Internet, and these dealers provide mail-order services:

Airguns of Arizona: AoA has been around for many years. Their interesting website is a frequent stop for me, containing a diverse product line of new and used airguns, plus scopes and accessories. There is also much useful information to peruse, including a very informative blog. While visiting the site, be sure to check out their Custom ACP Benjamin M-397 pump-up air rifle, among other custom airgun items.

Pomona Airguns: This California-based firm offers good old-fashioned one-on-one service. Steve has been in the business since 1978. That's long enough to know the ins and outs of many airgun systems, including pre-charged guns. He can tear them apart and fix them, along with other types like springers. The Pomona website was recently reconstructed, and shows just some of the many products and services. Be patient when calling, and you'll have an interesting conversation with a knowledgeable and friendly individual.

Pyramyd Air: Located in Ohio, Pyramyd Air continues to grow by leaps and bounds. They have an active social media presence, and a huge product line backed up by active marketing. Their detailed website is a gold mine for in-depth examination of numerous airguns and accessories. You'll even see links to owner's manuals and product-specific videos, along with a suitably named "Airgun Academy" authored by Tom Gaylord. PA's published customer reviews are another good source for product-specific information. So is their comprehensive pellet chart. Be sure to check them out.

Straight Shooters Precision Airguns, Inc.: Since its inception back in 1997, this Minnesota-based specialty airgun firm has been selling and testing a number of interesting airguns. One great service they offer is an "our take" tab. By opening an airgun description, viewers can click into an in-depth evaluation, complete with chronograph results. Velocity and energy results are shown at the muzzle, and also at 10, 25, and 50 yards. Nice! Beyond this feature, the whole site is worth your time.

Here are a few more well-established airgun dealers. Again, the list is probably not complete:

Airgun Depot: Utah-based firm in business since 2002, carrying a large product line.

Precision Airguns and Supplies: A well-named Michigan firm with a nice line of interesting airguns.

Precision Pellet: A long-time airgun dealer and warranty repair station located in Pennsylvania.

Topgun Airguns: Another Arizona-based company with a long history.

AIRGUN GUNSMITHS

Competent airgunsmiths can't be found on every street corner. While some of the above dealers offer repair services, sometimes an oddball or obsolete design requires a real specialist:

Alan Zasadny (847 838 0187): My son's pre-charged air rifle developed a leak. It's just old enough that service and parts were a problem. Alan came to the rescue and really went out of his way to make things right in a timely manner, despite personal scheduling conflicts. The gun soon reappeared in perfect working order, with a custom fill modification to boot.

INFORMATIONAL AIRGUN SOURCES

Here are a few intriguing sources for everything from general information to custom airgun builds, tuning, specialized accessories, and airgun hunting:

American Airguns website: This resource is a great way to link into nearly all aspects of the wide airgun field, from larger manufacturers to less well-known custom airgun smiths. Spend some time here and you'll see that this book only scratches the surface of a fascinating obsession. Any airgunners interested in custom tunes and personal servicing should definitely check out this site.

Hard Air Magazine: This online resource offers a buyer's guide, product reviews, airgun news, and links to other services.

Varmint Air's Airgun Hunting Blog: Those into airgun hunting will want to check this site out. It's a treasure trove of great information, including prairie dog shoots, PCP technologies, and other neat topics.

American Airgunner: How about a TV show dedicated exclusively to airguns? You'll find one on The Pursuit Channel. Topics include "The Round Table", a technical spot hosted by Rossi Morreali with airgun experts Tom Gaylord, Jim Chapman, and Rick Eutsler participating. Interesting hunting segments can be seen with Steve Criner, some of which involve big bore airguns. For those lacking channel access, the shows can also be seen through live streaming.

OTHER *SURVIVAL GUNS* TITLES

Survival Guns: A Beginner's Guide: This book is the first in the series, and serves as a guide to help build a firearm battery. It starts with a gun safe, to which firearms and accessories are added using a planned process. To help make the best choices, some key underlying principles are defined. From there, procurement of several essential systems can commence. A baseline inventory of a shotgun, two rifles, and a handgun serve as cornerstones. Further additions include some interesting specialty firearms and accessories. The firearms on the essentials list, as well as many other types, will be thoroughly covered in the series of system-specific manuals. In each, the various models, ammunition, and accessories will be closely examined. While this book is written for beginners, those familiar with firearms should find topics of value. The information will be detailed, covering far more than just a firearm itself.

Shotguns: A Comprehensive Guide: Would you like a bird gun, riot gun, and high-powered rifle all rolled into one single shotgun? Where's the tradeoff on recoil and performance? What shells work best with different chokes? This publication covers everything you ever wanted to know about shotguns. Technical aspects are explored, including the different types of guns, gauges, shells, chokes, shot sizes, and ballistics. Accessories are examined, along with training tips and other useful information. The human factor is addressed, with methods to accommodate smaller-statured shooters. Putting it all together, you'll not only have serious defensive capabilities, but also a means for the harvesting of both small game and very large animals. This shotgun manual shows you the way.

Rimfire Rifles: A Buyer's and Shooter's Guide: The key to understanding the entire rimfire system, from firearms… Well, your food stores won't last forever, and don't forget, they could also be lost. So, like it or not, some form of subsistence hunting just might be in the cards. In that case, the *right* tools will essential. Noise could be a concern, so for those who understand its full capabilities, a rimfire rifle just may be the perfect choice. Put the right load in the right rifle, and the loudest sound heard will be a bullet striking its target. The key is an understanding of the entire rimfire system, from firearms through calibers, and the many cartridge options. Since not every combination will work, knowledge is our key to success and a full belly. Good solid shooting ability counts as well, and a rimfire rifle is the perfect practice tool. Throw in a dash of defensive value, and we have a system worth a very close look. That's what this book is all about.

UPCOMING SURVIVAL GUNS FIREARM PUBLICATIONS

The Centerfire Rifle/AR-15 Manual: Are you interested in leverguns or semi-auto rifles? How about bolt-actions, or an entire family of guns in different calibers? How do you choose the right scope, and how do you sight it in? How do you select the most accurate loads, or pick the right bullets? How do you reduce recoil for younger shooters? Following in the steps of the rimfire & air gun manuals, the centerfire book takes us to the next level. Optics and ballistic aiming systems are explored, along with skill-building regimens. You'll see methods to assess true accuracy, and other useful tips. Different calibers and loads are discussed, as are various rifle choices. The AR-15 has grown wildly popular, with dozens of brands and hundreds of accessories to choose from. It's an extremely versatile platform for good reason, and can be instantly transformed to many different profiles. Switch-top conversions are possible in .22 LR, through several pistol calibers, and serious big-bore rounds. On top of that, universal "Picatinny" mounting points will easily accommodate nearly unlimited optical or equipment choices. Since most of us don't have unlimited funds, we'll need to determine exactly *which* accessories are necessary. This edition is the next progression in our system-based approach for development of a practical firearms battery.

The Handgun Manual: You can shoot yourself with the wrong combination of pistol, holster and clothing, so which ones are dangerous? You may understand the fundamentals of shooting, but how do they apply to handguns? Are you interested in a 1911 pistol? If so, did you know you can create your own multi-caliber pistol off a single frame? What about other types? Which loads are your best defensive choices? This publication covers everything you'll need to know about handguns, from different models through practical calibers, holsters, and accessories. You'll see some interesting alternatives to six-shot revolvers and the latest high-capacity pistols. The smaller guns are covered, too. Practical revolver and pistol skills are detailed, along with recommended practice regimens. *The Handgun Manual* rolls all of this information into one source for safe and effective handling.